Justice at Work

Legal Framework to a Safer Workplace for Women

Written By

Sunitha Bhagyalakshmi

Edited By

Roopashri Sinha

Contents _Toc174372676

Acknowledgements

Writing this book, *Justice at Work: Legal Framework to a Safer Workplace for Women*, has been an incredible experience. I am deeply grateful to all the individuals who have supported and inspired me throughout this journey.

My special thanks to my husband and my children, Karthik and Kaushal, who always motivate me to achieve newer heights. You have been my pillars of strength, and I am forever indebted to the Almighty for bringing each of you into my life.

I am grateful to all the Gurus and mentors in my life, especially Dr Aparna Sethi, for starting me on my journey in POSH Consultancy, which shaped my future.

I would like to give a special thanks to my exceptional Book coach, Roopashri Sinha, whose guidance and expertise have been indispensable in refining my ideas and transforming them into the written words you now hold. It would have taken many years to publish without her support. I would like to mention a special thanks to Miss Vandana, whose keen editorial eye and thoughtful feedback have pushed me to deliver a book that I am truly proud of.

Once again, I thank each one of those whom I unintentionally must not have mentioned here explicitly but who have touched my life in some way.

Lastly, I am grateful to the Universe, all my well-wishers and strangers who helped me directly or indirectly and most importantly, to this book's readers and supporters.

With immense gratitude,

Sunitha Bhagyalakshmi

Straight from the Author's Heart

When I began writing Justice at Work: Legal Framework to a Safer Workplace for Women, I was driven by a singular vision: to create a comprehensive, insightful, and practical guide for navigating the complexities of the Prevention of Sexual Harassment (POSH) law in India. Having spent years working closely with various organisations and witnessing first-hand the challenges they face in implementing these vital regulations, I felt a profound responsibility to share my knowledge and experiences.

This book is designed to be more than just a manual; it is a resource, a companion, and a source of empowerment for those tasked with ensuring safe and respectful workplaces. It delves into the nuances of POSH investigations, offering detailed guidance on everything from the legal framework to the procedures. It also includes many ready-to-use forms, sample templates, and sample notices that Internal Committees can follow in handling complaints with sensitivity and fairness.

Throughout the chapters, I have included fictitious yet realistic scenarios inspired by actual cases. These stories aim to bring to life the often-abstract principles of POSH, making them relatable and more straightforward to comprehend. By illustrating key points with these narratives, I hope to provide a clearer picture of the law's real-world application and the impact it can have on individuals and organisations alike.

As you turn these pages, you will find a blend of legal insights, practical tips, and heartfelt reflections. I aim to equip you with the tools to perform your duties effectively and empathetically. Whether you are an HR professional, a member of an Internal Committee, or a leader committed to fostering a safe work environment, this book is for you.

Writing this book has been a labour of love, and I am deeply grateful for the support and encouragement of my colleagues, friends, and family. Your trust has fuelled my determination to create a work that stands up to the challenges and responsibilities we face in promoting justice at work.

Thank you for joining me on this crucial journey. Together, we can make a difference.

Warm regards,

Sunitha Bhagyalakshmi

Editor's Note

The book ***Justice at Work: Legal Framework to a Safer Workplace for Women*** is a comprehensive guide for readers who deal with the subject matter. Living a different perspective of the law and its approach gave me immense joy. The readers will witness the author's expertise and experience throughout the book.

While the author has taken every care to bring the correct information to the readers, as an editor, I have worked on the book's general English and the literature's scope enhancement. The author has confirmed the authenticity of the sources and has a disclaimer about using AI writing wherever it is useful, keeping the personal touch intact. The images inside the book are AI-generated to give the best understanding of the subject.

It is a privilege to present a work that enlightens and empowers readers to navigate their path to success with integrity, strategy, and mindset.

Love

Roopashri Sinha

A global Author Mentor
https://www.facebook.com/mentor.roopashri.sinha
https://www.linkedin.com/in/authorroopashrisinha

Chapter 1:

Understanding POSH and Its Importance

Introduction

Creating a safe and respectful workplace is more than just a legal requirement; it's a personal commitment to creating a workplace where everyone feels valued and protected. The significance of the Prevention of Sexual Harassment (POSH) Act, 2013 extends beyond its sections and rules, it's about the organisational culture and the genuine sense of security that each employee experiences.

As a POSH External Member, I have not just had the privilege but, at times, the challenge of witnessing the insightful impact of POSH on workplace dynamics. There was this one incident which is still fresh in my mind. The procedural compliance was nothing short of exemplary. Every guideline was meticulously adhered to, and the documentation was impeccable. But beneath this veneer of compliance was a culture steeped in fear and mistrust. Employees, particularly women, felt unsupported and unheard despite the presence of formal processes. This experience was a stark reminder that while procedural compliance is crucial, it is insufficient. True change requires addressing the human and cultural aspects that form the bedrock of a safe workplace.

This chapter will explore the core elements of the POSH Act of 2013, highlighting the importance of genuine compliance and the cultural shift needed to protect and empower employees truly.

Overview of the POSH Act, 2013

In my interaction with various IC members, I've often encountered organisations that take great pride in their adherence to the POSH Act 2013. This section will provide an overall view of the Act's objective, definitions, and some significant sections. I recall an instance where a company, confident in its compliance, was stunned to learn that many of its employees were unaware of the Act's specifics and what behaviours were considered sexual harassment. This incident emphasised the importance of continuous awareness and refresher training programs for the employees, ensuring they understand their rights and the protections available under the Act.

The POSH Act of 2013 is more than just a set of rules; it's a framework designed to create a respectful and safe work environment. By understanding its provisions, organisations can better implement policies that genuinely protect their employees.

The POSH Act of 2013 is a comprehensive piece of legislation designed to prevent sexual harassment in the workplace. It defines sexual harassment, outlines employers' responsibilities, and mandates forming an Internal Committee (IC) to handle complaints. Key provisions include:

- Definition of sexual harassment, including physical contact, demands for sexual favours, sexually coloured remarks, and other unwelcome physical, verbal, or non-verbal conduct.

- Employers' obligations to provide a safe working environment, display information about the Act, and organise awareness programs.

- Establish an Internal Committee with ten or more employees at every branch or office to address complaints.

Importance of Compliance and the Impact of POSH on Workplace Culture

Proper compliance with the POSH Act is about more than following procedures; it's about bringing respect and inclusivity into workplace culture. I remember a case where a company's HR department had flawless procedures on paper, yet the office culture was very toxic. Employees felt isolated and fearful of reporting sexual harassment, worrying about potential retaliation. This incident made me think deeply, looking for solutions that led me to delve into and discuss how genuine compliance with POSH guidelines fosters a positive workplace culture, enhances employee morale, and boosts organisational reputation.

Organisations can cultivate a culture of trust and respect by creating an environment where employees feel safe speaking up and assured of support. This cultural shift protects employees and drives overall business success, as a happy, respected workforce is productive.

Compliance with the POSH Act is essential for creating a respectful and inclusive workplace culture. Proper implementation of the Act helps in:

Ensuring employees feel safe and supported enhances their morale and productivity.

Build a reputation as a fair and responsible employer that can attract and retain top talent.

Reducing the risk of workplace conflicts and fostering a positive working environment.

Legal Ramifications of Non-Compliance

The consequences of non-compliance with the POSH Act are severe and far-reaching. Through my experiences, I have seen organisations face hefty fines[1], reputational damage, and even criminal charges due to lapses in their POSH procedures. In a recent case, *Gayatri Balaswamy v. ISG Novasoft Technologies Ltd.*, the Madras HC levied a heavy penalty of INR 1.68 crores on the company for not having complied with the employer's mandate under the POSH Act 2013, including the non-establishment of the IC. The court said that in its findings the non-compliance on the part of the organisation caused great distress to the survivor of sexual harassment (petitioner).

---

[1] Gayatri Balaswamy v. ISG Novasoft Technologies Ltd., 2014 SCC OnLine Mad 6568: (2015) 1 Mad LJ 5.

In another similar case, a company that was only giving importance to its reputation had to face legal action after it had ignored a series of harassment complaints. Now, I will discuss the legal implications of non-compliance, emphasising the importance of proactive measures and diligent adherence to the Act.

Understanding the legal consequences is crucial for any organisation. This is a stark reminder that neglecting POSH mandates can lead to serious repercussions, affecting the company's reputation and standing in the industry and a loss of employees' trust.

By weaving these personal stories and experiences of other POSH committee members into the book, I aim to provide insights into the POSH Act and many practical tips for handling sexual harassment scenarios.

Organisations must think and act beyond procedural compliance to create a workplace where employees feel safe, respected, and valued.

Non-compliance with the POSH Act can lead to severe legal consequences, including:

Monetary penalties imposed by regulatory bodies for failing to implement the Act's provisions.

Reputational damage resulting from publicised harassment cases and inadequate handling of complaints.

Potential criminal charges against individuals responsible for neglecting their duties under the Act. Understanding these legal implications underscores the importance of strict adherence to the POSH guidelines to protect the organisation and its employees.

Chapter 2:

Identifying the Problem and its Complexities

Role of IC Members

Ensuring a safe workplace is challenging, especially for all the Internal Committee (IC) members responsible for handling POSH investigations. The role of IC members is quasi-judicial, and further, Section 11 (3) of the POSH Act also grants IC the same powers vested in a Civil Court under the Code of Civil Procedure, 1908. IC Committee members have the right to summon and enforce the attendance of any person examined on oath and undertake all actions requiring discovery and production of documents. A Division Bench of the Delhi High Court2 Pronounced that the Presiding Officers and Members of IC are also 'Judges' within the meaning of Section 19 of the Indian Penal Code, 1960. These individuals often find themselves navigating many challenges of legal intricacies and procedural hurdles which can be overwhelming and daunting.

As a POSH External Member, I've heard from some of the experienced people from my fraternity who witnessed these challenges first-hand. One particular experience stands out: an IC member from a reputable organisation struggled to understand the legal framework surrounding a complex harassment case. Despite having the best intentions, the lack of clarity and confidence in handling the procedures led to delays and increased tension among the involved parties. This situation underscored the critical need for thorough training and support for IC members to manage such sensitive investigations effectively.

Through my acquaintances in the corporate world, I've gained invaluable wisdom on the importance of balancing legal knowledge with empathy and cultural sensitivity. In this chapter, I will explore some of the

---

2 Neeraj Bala v. Union of India, W.P.(C)-6712/2021.

common challenges faced in POSH investigations and the stakes involved and provide real-life examples to illustrate these complexities.

Common Challenges in POSH Investigations

Internal Committee members often encounter countless challenges when conducting POSH investigations. This is because each POSH case is unique as the people involved are different, and the subjectivity of the situation is involved. What works for one organisation may not work for another; hence, the IC members will have to keep an open mind to handle every investigation on a case-to-case basis. Some of the challenges faced by IC members include:

Understanding Legal Frameworks: The POSH Act, 2013 is a comprehensive and intricate legislation. IC members, especially those without a legal background, often struggle to understand its definitions, provisions, and procedural requirements fully. This can lead to confusion and errors in the investigation process.

Handling Sensitive Information: Sexual harassment cases involve highly sensitive information. IC members must ensure confidentiality is maintained at all times to protect the privacy of the complainant, the respondent and the witnesses. However, managing this information discreetly and conducting a thorough investigation can be challenging.

Ensuring Impartiality: Bias, whether conscious or unconscious, can affect the fairness of an investigation. IC members may find it difficult to remain completely impartial, especially in cases involving colleagues or senior executives. Ensuring a fair and unbiased investigation process is crucial for serving justice.

Emotional Strain: Sexual harassment cases can be emotionally taxing for all parties involved. IC members, too, may experience emotional strain, impacting their ability to conduct objective and effective investigations. Providing emotional support and training on handling such cases is essential.

I recall an instance shared by an External member where an IC member was unsure how to proceed with a case involving a senior executive, fearing potential repercussions. This highlighted the need for clear guidelines and support systems to help IC members navigate such scenarios confidently.

The Stakes Involved for IC Members

The consequences of failing to identify and address the complexities of POSH investigations are significant and can have serious consequences for IC members. These include but are not limited to:

Legal Accountability: IC members are legally obligated to conduct thorough and impartial investigations. Failure to comply with the POSH Act can lead to legal consequences for the IC members personally, including fines and potential legal action. In severe cases, IC members could face criminal charges for negligence or misconduct in handling cases if their order is challenged in the court.

Reputational Damage: IC members are often seen as the custodians of fairness and justice of the POSH committee in an organization. Mishandling a POSH investigation can tarnish their personal reputation, making it difficult for them to maintain the trust and respect of their colleagues and the broader professional community.

Professional Consequences: Inadequate handling of POSH cases can affect an IC member's career prospects. They may face disciplinary action from their employer, including demotion or termination. Additionally, their ability to serve on other internal committees or in similar roles in the future could be compromised.

Emotional and Psychological Impact: The emotional toll of dealing with sensitive and potentially traumatic cases can be significant. IC members who do not have the necessary support and training may experience stress, anxiety, and burnout, affecting their overall well-being and performance.

Impact on Workplace Culture: IC members play a crucial role in shaping the organization's response to sexual harassment. Poorly managed investigations can contribute to a toxic work environment, where employees feel unsafe and unsupported. This, in turn, can lead to low morale, high turnover, and a decline in productivity.

In one notable case, an IC member faced immense personal and professional backlash after failing to address a harassment complaint appropriately. The situation not only resulted in legal action against the company but also severely damaged the IC member's reputation and career. It became a stark reminder of the importance of diligence, empathy, and thoroughness in handling POSH investigations.

Real-Life Examples and Case Studies

Real-life examples and case studies provide invaluable insights into the complexities of POSH investigations. These stories are from not only my experiences but also other experienced POSH IC members and External members which bring to light the diverse challenges and solutions, offering practical lessons for IC members.

Case Study 1: A multinational corporation faced a high-profile sexual harassment case involving a senior executive. The company's IC, initially overwhelmed by the legal intricacies, sought support from External IC advice and conducted thorough training sessions for its members. By balancing legal compliance with emotional support for the complainant, the IC managed to resolve the case effectively. This highlighted the importance of continuous learning and External IC member support in handling complex cases.

Case Study 2: A small business with limited resources faced significant criticism after mishandling a harassment complaint. The IC, lacking proper training, failed to maintain confidentiality and appeared biased in their investigation. This resulted in legal action, reputational damage, and a toxic work environment. The case emphasized the critical need for proper training and adherence to POSH guidelines, regardless of the organisation's size.

Case Study 3: An IC member's personal journey from uncertainty to confidence in handling cases showcases the transformative power of comprehensive training and support. Initially struggling with the procedural aspects of POSH investigations, the member attended specialized workshops and sought mentorship from experienced POSH professionals. Over time, this member became a proficient and empathetic investigator, highlighting the importance of ongoing education and support.

Case Study 4: A mid-sized tech firm faced an internal scandal when multiple harassment complaints were filed against a popular team leader. The IC, inexperienced in dealing with such high volumes of cases, initially became fearful of handling the investigation. They decided to take the assistance of their experienced External IC member for guidance. This decision not only helped streamline the process but also provided an impartial perspective, ensuring fairness and transparency. The successful resolution of these cases led to the implementation of a more robust training program for all IC members.

Case Study 5: In a large manufacturing company, an IC member found themselves under immense pressure to close a harassment case quickly to avoid bad press. However, the member insisted on a thorough investigation despite the pressure. The detailed investigation uncovered general issues in the company's culture, leading to comprehensive reforms. This case highlighted the importance of integrity and thoroughness, even under pressure.

Case Study 6: A financial services company faced a complex case involving cultural differences and alleged harassment. The IC members struggled to investigate given the cultural sensitivities involved. By consulting with cultural experts and conducting extensive interviews, the IC managed to handle the case delicately and fairly. This case emphasized the importance of cultural awareness and sensitivity in POSH investigations.

Case Study 7: An IC member in a retail company encountered a situation where the complainant was hesitant to provide details due to fear of retaliation. The IC member, trained in empathetic communication, managed to build trust and encouraged the complainant to share details of the harassment. This case emphasised the importance of empathy and trust-building in effectively handling sensitive cases, especially where the Complainant is fearful to come forward and raise a formal complaint.

Case Study 8: A hospitality firm faced a high-profile harassment case that gathered a lot of media attention. The IC, prepared for such scenarios, managed media relations carefully and ensured the investigation was conducted transparently yet confidentially. The positive handling of the situation not only resolved the case but also reinforced the company's commitment to a safe workplace. This case highlighted the importance of media management and transparency.

Case Study 9: An IC in an educational institution dealt with a harassment case involving students and faculty members. The complexity of navigating power dynamics between students and faculty posed a significant challenge. By involving representation from both students and senior faculty members in the IC committee and maintaining strict confidentiality, the IC managed to resolve the case fairly. This case illustrated the unique challenges educational institutions face and the importance of impartiality.

Case Study 10: In a government organization, an IC member faced resistance from colleagues who were sceptical about the importance of POSH training. The IC member took the initiative to educate their peers about the significance of a safe workplace through organising workshops and seminars. Over time, this led to a cultural shift within the organization, promoting a more respectful and supportive environment. This case taught the importance of support and continuous training in promoting POSH awareness.

Case Study 11: In a large healthcare organization, an IC member dealt with a harassment case involving medical staff and patients. The IC faced challenges in maintaining patient confidentiality while ensuring a thorough investigation. By coordinating with all the parties involved in a very professional way, the IC managed to handle the case effectively, highlighting the need for interdisciplinary collaboration in complex scenarios.

Case Study 12: An IC in an advertising agency encountered a case where the accused was a client. The IC had to balance the need for a fair investigation with maintaining the client relationship. The case was handled with utmost professionalism, ensuring justice was served without jeopardizing the business relationship.

Case Study 13: A construction firm faced multiple harassment complaints from female workers. The IC, predominantly male due to the absence of women employees in the organisation initially struggled to understand the perspectives of the complainants. By bringing in the involvement of female IC members from their sister concern and conducting sensitivity training, the IC was able to approach the cases more empathetically and effectively.

Case Study 14: In a non-profit organization, an IC member dealt with a harassment case involving volunteers. The short nature of volunteer work posed challenges in gathering evidence and testimonies. The IC used creative solutions like virtual interviews and anonymous reporting mechanisms to handle the case, highlighting the need for flexibility in handling each case on an individual basis.

Case Study 15: An IC member in a media company faced a situation where the complainant was a whistle-blower who exposed general harassment. The IC had to navigate the complexities of protecting the whistle-blower while addressing the widespread issue. This case indicated the importance of robust whistle-blower protection policies in every organisation.

Case Study 16: A start-up with a flat organizational structure faced a harassment case involving co-founders. The IC had to navigate the power dynamics and potential conflicts of interest. But the IC along with External member ensured a fair and unbiased investigation, leading to a resolution that preserved the start up's integrity.

Case Study 17: An IC in a transportation company dealt with a case involving harassment during work travel. The IC had to understand the jurisdictional issues and company policies related to travel. By clarifying policies and ensuring support mechanisms during travel, the IC managed to address the case effectively.

Case Study 18: In a consulting firm, the IC members handled a harassment case involving a high-profile client and an employee. The complexity of maintaining client confidentiality while ensuring employee safety was the biggest challenge in this case. The IC navigated this by setting clear boundaries and involving External IC in every step of the investigation to arrive an unbiased decision-making process.

Case Study 19: A retail chain faced a harassment case involving seasonal workers. The IC had to adapt their approach to handle the temporary nature of the workforce. By implementing rapid response mechanisms and providing immediate support, the IC managed to resolve the case efficiently.

Case Study 20: An IC in a research institution encountered a case where the complainant was a foreign national. The IC had to navigate cultural differences and language barriers. By involving cultural liaisons and providing translation services, the IC ensured a fair investigation process and instilled the confidence in all the members of the research institution.

Through these examples, I aim to provide IC members with relatable scenarios and actionable insights to enhance their understanding and handling of POSH investigations. By sharing these experiences and the wisdom gained from them, this section seeks to equip IC members with the knowledge and confidence to navigate the complexities of POSH investigations effectively. Though effort has been made to provide as many scenarios here it is the practical application of expertise and continuous training that can help IC members use their subjective judgment in handling different scenarios. The identity and names of Organizations and IC members have not been mentioned in the above cases in order to ensure strict compliance with confidentiality.

Chapter 3:

Practical Solutions for Effective Investigations

Practical Overview

Reflecting on my journey and interactions with many experts in the POSH arena, I vividly remember the moment when everything clicked. The complainant felt unheard of during a particularly challenging case, and the respondent was equally frustrated. The investigation seemed to be heading nowhere, with tensions running high. In this chaos, I realised the importance of being a problem-solver.

This realisation was transformative. I understood that my role wasn't just about following procedures but providing clear, practical guidance to effectively navigate the complexities of POSH investigations. It was about ensuring that every voice was heard, every fact was considered, and every action was fair and compliant. In this section, I aim to share that understanding with you, offering practical solutions to help you become a problem-solver in your own right.

Step-by-step guide to conducting POSH investigations

Conducting a POSH investigation can be daunting, but breaking it down into manageable steps can make the process more approachable and effective. Here's a step-by-step guide based on my experiences:

Step 1: Receiving the Complaint

The initial step involves receiving the complaint. Upon receipt of the complaint, IC has to ensure some important elements to establish sexual harassment, such as the respondent displaying improper behaviour, the complainant experiencing harm, and the behaviour occurring at the workplace or any work-related event. IC members should also evaluate the Service Rules, Workplace policies, Vishakha Guidelines and any related laws that may be applicable. Ensure that the complainant feels comfortable and supported. This may involve offering reassurance about confidentiality and protection against retaliation. For instance, in one case, a complainant was hesitant to come forward due to fear of retaliation. By providing a safe and confidential environment, we encouraged openness and trust. Documenting the complaint accurately and comprehensively at this stage is also crucial. The Presiding Officer (PO) has to issue an acknowledgement to the Complainant for receipt of the complaint. **(See sample POSH Complaint Form Template)**

Step 2: Preliminary Inquiry

Conduct a preliminary inquiry to determine the validity of the complaint and whether it falls under the purview of the POSH Act, along with all the internal policies and employment agreements of the parties involved. This involves understanding the nature of the complaint and gathering initial information. For example, a complaint may not initially seem to qualify as harassment, but a deeper assessment could reveal underlying issues that need addressing. During this stage, it's essential to evaluate the context, the severity of the allegations, and any immediate actions required to protect the complainant. At times general harassment is misunderstood to be sexual harassment and vice versa. After completion of the initial discussion with both the complainant and the respondent, IC should explore options for formal or informal resolution depending on the gravity of the harassment. An important point to note here is after informing both the processes available for redressal of the complaint, the choice of formal or informal process rests only with the complainant. If the complainant opts for formal redressal or the IC members decide to take the complaint formally, given the gravity of the harassment, then the formal investigation process begins.

Step 3: Issuing Notice to Complainant, Respondent, and Witnesses

After the preliminary inquiry, the first step is to inform the respondent in writing within seven days of receiving the complaint that a complaint has been received against him by attaching a copy of the complaint. The next step is to issue formal notices to the complainant, respondent, and the witnesses mentioning the date and time of the interview. This step is crucial for informing all parties involved about the investigation and ensuring their participation. The PO should clearly outline the allegations and the investigation process and emphasize confidentiality. It is important to note that the IC members are unbiased and trained in handling such cases. Also, if there is any conflict of interest, such as the complainant or respondent is a close friend of any of the IC members, then that member should step down from the investigation, and a new IC should be nominated by following due process. In one memorable case, excluding an IC member who was a close friend of the respondent was crucial in ensuring that the complainant felt comfortable and supported throughout the investigation. This diverse and trained IC team can help maintain a balanced perspective and ensure a fair process. **(See sample POSH Investigation Notice Template for Complaint and Respondent)**

Step 4: Planning the Investigation

Develop a clear plan outlining the steps to be taken, including who will be interviewed, what documents need to be reviewed, and the timeline. Detailed planning helps streamline the process and avoid unnecessary delays. For example, a well-structured plan can identify key individuals to interview and critical evidence to review, ensuring a thorough investigation. Establishing clear objectives and timelines is essential for maintaining focus and efficiency.

Step 5: Conducting Interviews

Conduct interviews with the complainant, the respondent, and witnesses, if any, specified by both parties. Ensure that the interviews are conducted in a confidential and respectful manner by ensuring that none of the parties come face to face during the interview process. If the witnesses choose to remain anonymous, especially those specified by the complainant, then ensure that their identity is kept confidential. When the witness/witnesses of the complainant choose to remain anonymous, the respondent can cross-examine only through a written questionnaire. During one investigation, the respondent was initially defensive, but through respectful and empathetic questioning, we were able to gather valuable information. Use open-ended questions and avoid leading questions to ensure the interviews yield comprehensive and unbiased information. (See sample POSH Investigation Complaint, Respondent and Witness Interview Template)

Step 6: Reviewing Evidence

Review all available evidence, including emails, messages, and other relevant documents. Electronic evidence corroborated the complainant's account in a particular case, leading to a fair resolution. It's important to be thorough and objective in examining all evidence, ensuring nothing is overlooked.

Step 7: Analysis and Findings

Analyse the information gathered and document the findings. Ensure that the analysis is objective and based on facts. It is important to note that the IC should ensure that the case and the investigation are conducted considering the facts and findings and not in an emotional manner. In one investigation, meticulous analysis of the evidence led to uncovering patterns of behaviour that were critical in reaching a fair conclusion. Identifying any inconsistencies or corroborations in the testimonies and evidence can help bring the facts of the case to the surface, thereby ensuring fairness and following the principles of natural justice as enshrined in the Act. (See sample POSH Investigation Checklist for IC)

Step 8: Preparing the Report

Prepare a detailed report outlining the findings, conclusions, reasoning and recommendations. The report should be clear, concise, and free from omissions of vital details. A well-documented report is instrumental in ensuring that the recommendations are implemented effectively. In one case, the clarity and thoroughness of the report were crucial to the successful implementation of the recommendations. (See sample POSH Investigation Report Template)

Step 9: Decision and Action

Based on the report, the Internal Committee (IC) should decide on the appropriate actions. This may include disciplinary action, counselling, or policy changes. In a notable case, the decision led to significant policy changes that improved the workplace environment. It's important that the actions taken are proportionate to the findings and aimed at preventing future occurrences.

Step 10: Follow-up and Monitoring

Ensure that the recommended actions are implemented and monitor the situation to prevent recurrence. Follow-up is crucial in maintaining trust and ensuring a safe workplace. In one instance, regular follow-up helped rebuild trust and foster a positive workplace culture. This includes checking in with the complainant to ensure their well-being and monitoring the workplace environment to ensure that the issues do not recur.

Ensuring Fairness and Compliance in the Investigation Process

Fairness and compliance are the cornerstones of an effective POSH investigation. Here's how to ensure both:

Maintaining Impartiality: Ensure that all IC members are unbiased and impartial. This can be challenging, especially in cases involving colleagues or friends. In one investigation, an IC member had a personal connection with the respondent, which was addressed by replacing the IC member to ensure impartiality.

Adhering to Legal Guidelines: Follow the legal guidelines outlined in the POSH Act, 2013, HR policies and any other relevant applicable Acts. This includes maintaining confidentiality, conducting timely investigations, and supporting the complainant. In a particular case, strict adherence to the legal guidelines was crucial in defending the organisation against potential legal action brimming from multiple harassment complaints.

Providing Support: Offer support to both the complainant and the respondent. This can include counselling services, ensuring confidentiality, and providing a safe environment. I recall a case where emotional support to the complainant was crucial in helping them navigate the investigation process.

Training and Awareness: Regular training and awareness programs for IC members and employees can help them understand the importance of fairness and compliance. In one organization, regular training sessions led to a noticeable improvement in the handling of POSH cases and a reduction in the number of complaints received previously.

Documentation and Record-Keeping: Maintain thorough documentation of all steps taken during the investigation. This not only ensures compliance but also provides a clear record in case of future disputes. In one memorable case, detailed documentation was instrumental in defending the IC's decisions during an external audit.

Tools and Resources for IC Members

Having the right tools and resources can make a significant difference in the effectiveness of POSH investigations. POSH investigations require a blend of legal knowledge, practical skills, and the right tools to ensure thorough and fair outcomes. IC members tasked with conducting these investigations benefit greatly from leveraging various resources to enhance their effectiveness. I have tried to explore essential tools and resources that can aid IC members in their crucial work, drawing from practical experiences and best practices. Here are some that have proven invaluable in my experience:

Legal Handbooks and Guides: Comprehensive legal handbooks and guides provide clarity on the POSH Act and its provisions. These resources ensure that IC members are well-versed in the legal framework governing sexual harassment in the workplace. For instance, I've often relied on these handbooks to verify procedural steps and ensure that our investigations align with legal requirements. Detailed explanations of legal terms, case studies, and step-by-step guides within these handbooks can serve as invaluable references during investigations.

Training Programs: Regular training programs for IC members are crucial in building the necessary skills and knowledge to handle POSH cases effectively. These programs often cover topics such as interviewing techniques, evidence evaluation, and maintaining confidentiality. In one organization, intensive training sessions dramatically improved the IC's handling of cases, equipping members with the confidence and competence needed to manage sensitive investigations. Such programs can also include mock investigations, role-playing scenarios, and updates on recent legal amendments.

Technology Tools: Utilizing technology tools for documentation, communication, and evidence gathering can significantly streamline the investigation process. For example, an online case management system can help track the progress of investigations and maintain confidentiality. Having case management tools can assist in organizing documents, scheduling interviews, and securely storing evidence, making the process more efficient and less prone to errors. Other technology tools, such as secure communication platforms and digital evidence collection tools can further enhance the IC's capabilities. Utilising technology tools for documentation, communication, and evidence gathering can streamline the investigation process.

External Experts and Consultants: Engaging external experts and consultants can provide an unbiased perspective and additional expertise. In several cases, the involvement of external IC members was crucial in ensuring a fair and thorough investigation.

Support Networks: Building a support network, including legal advisors, counsellors, and other IC members, can provide additional resources and an unbiased approach to the investigation process. I've found that having a robust support network has been invaluable in navigating complex cases.

Awareness Materials: Providing awareness materials, such as brochures, posters, and online resources, can help educate employees about their rights and responsibilities under the POSH Act. In one instance, a well-designed awareness campaign significantly increased the reporting and resolution of harassment cases.

By sharing these practical solutions and resources, I aim to equip IC members with the knowledge and tools needed to conduct effective POSH investigations. The goal is to foster a workplace environment that is safe, respectful, and compliant with legal standards, ensuring

that every voice is heard and every case is handled with
the utmost fairness and diligence.

Chapter 4:

Beyond Procedures: The Need for Cultural Shift

Proactive or Reactive

I am a strong believer in proactive measures rather than reactive ones in handling POSH issues. One of my friends, who is also a POSH consultant, shared that once she witnessed a case where the company was not taking many steps to educate their employees on sexual harassment because there were no harassment cases reported in the past two years. The company was trying to save costs on training, and what my friend found out was that the employees were hesitant to come forward with their complaints, and even when they did, the response was often defensive rather than supportive. This experience highlighted a vital truth: handling POSH issues effectively requires more than just compliance with procedures. It demands a proactive approach, fostering a culture of respect and safety, where every member of the organization feels valued and protected.

I recall a specific instance where an employee came forward with a harassment complaint. Despite having a robust policy framework, the company struggled with implementation. The leadership was disengaged, and the IC members were ill-prepared to handle the complexities of the case. This highlighted the pressing need for a cultural shift within the organization—a shift that prioritizes proactive measures over-reactive responses, ensuring that respect and safety are deeply embedded in the organizational ethos.

Leadership Commitment and Embedding Core Values

I've learned from my experiences that the tone at the top is critical in shaping organizational culture. In one memorable case shared by my friend, a company's leadership was deeply committed to fostering a safe and respectful workplace. They regularly communicated their dedication to POSH principles, not just during mandatory training sessions but through everyday actions and decisions. This commitment infused the entire organization with creating an environment where employees felt confident and supported in reporting issues.

Leadership should visibly support POSH initiatives and participate in training sessions. They should also regularly discuss the importance of a respectful workplace in meetings and communications. Frequent communication from leaders, including emails, town hall meetings, and internal newsletters, emphasizes the importance of POSH principles. Highlighting success stories and lessons learned from POSH cases can reinforce this commitment.

POSH principles should be explicitly stated in the company's mission, vision, and core values. Regularly revisiting these statements ensures they reflect current practices and goals. Decisions, from hiring to promotions, must reflect a commitment to a respectful workplace. Incorporating POSH principles into performance reviews and reward systems further embeds these values into the company culture.

Transparent Communication and Continuous Education

I have seen the profound impact of transparent communication and continuous education on workplace culture. In one organisation, the management established an open-door policy, encouraging employees to voice their concerns without fear of retaliation. They also implemented continuous education programs, ensuring that all employees, from entry-level to executive, understood the nuances of the POSH Act and their role in maintaining a safe workplace.

Creating channels for open communication, such as anonymous reporting systems and regular feedback sessions, fosters a culture of transparency. Issues should be addressed promptly, and regular updates on the status of complaints should be provided while maintaining confidentiality. Using multiple communication platforms ensures the message reaches everyone.

Ongoing training programs tailored to different levels of the organization are essential. Regular training sessions for all employees, including specialized training for managers and IC members, keep everyone informed and prepared. Updating training materials frequently to reflect the latest legal developments and best practices is crucial. Interactive methods such as role-playing, scenario-based learning, and e-learning modules make training more engaging and effective. Encouraging participation and feedback ensures the training is relevant and impactful.

Empowering IC and Benchmarking Best Practices

In my experience, empowering IC is crucial for effective POSH implementation. In one particular organisation, the IC members were given specialized training and resources, enabling them to handle investigations with competence and sensitivity. Additionally, the company benchmarked its practices against industry leaders, continuously improving its approach to POSH issues.

Providing IC members with specialized training in handling POSH cases, including legal aspects, interviewing techniques, and psychological support, ensures they are well-prepared. Regular refresher courses and advanced training keep their skills up-to-date. Access to necessary resources, such as legal counsel, psychological experts, and investigation tools, is critical. Allocating a dedicated budget for IC operations ensures they can perform their duties effectively.

Regularly benchmarking POSH practices against industry leaders and standards helps organisations stay updated. Participating in industry forums, seminars, and workshops provides valuable insights into the latest trends and innovations. Identifying best practices from other organizations and adapting them to fit the company's context ensures continuous improvement. Implementing a feedback loop allows for regular review and refinement of practices based on new insights and lessons learned.

Industry Best Practices:

Specialized Training for IC Members:

Ensuring consistent and comprehensive training for all IC members is essential. Keeping training materials up-to-date with the latest legal developments and best practices ensures the training is relevant. Providing ongoing training for IC members and other stakeholders to keep them updated on the latest best practices at least once a year is necessary. Develop a culture of learning and development, emphasising the importance of staying current with industry standards.

Developing a standardized training program with regular updates and refreshers helps maintain consistency. Organizations should utilize technology to streamline and automate POSH processes. Industry leaders can look at implementing POSH case management systems to track complaints, investigations, and resolutions efficiently. Also, partnering with external experts for training sessions enhances the quality of training.

Access to Resources:

Providing the necessary tools and resources for IC members to perform their duties effectively is critical. Ensuring timely access to legal and psychological support is also important.

Allocating a dedicated budget for IC resources and establishing partnerships with external service providers for additional support ensures IC members have what they need.

Benchmarking Best Practices:

Staying updated with the latest best practices and integrating them into existing frameworks can be challenging. Balancing the adoption of new practices with the organization's existing culture and systems requires careful planning.

Establishing partnerships with industry leaders and participating in regular knowledge-sharing forums helps stay informed. Implementing a continuous improvement process and regularly reviewing and updating practices based on feedback and new insights ensures practices remain effective and relevant.

By undertaking proactive measures and fostering a culture of respect and safety, organizations can move beyond mere procedural compliance to truly embody the principles of the POSH Act. This cultural shift not only protects employees but also enhances the overall health and productivity of the workplace.

Chapter 5:

Addressing Common Concerns and Fears

Problem solver mindset

I always advise the IC members to follow a problem-solver approach to sensitive investigations and maintaining confidentiality. During my tenure I encountered a particularly delicate case involving a high-ranking executive accused of harassment. The complainant, a young employee, was terrified of the potential fallout, both professionally and personally. The respondent, on the other hand, was equally distressed about the impact on his reputation and family. This case made me understand the critical need for handling sensitive investigations with utmost care and maintaining strict confidentiality.

In this situation, I had to adopt a problem-solver mindset, focusing on fair and impartial investigation techniques while providing psychological support to both parties. I realized the importance of not just addressing the immediate issue but also nurturing trust amongst both parties by demonstrating that their concerns would be handled with the highest level of integrity and sensitivity and by following the principles of natural justice as enshrined in the POSH Act. This experience highlighted the significance of providing psychological support and counselling, not just for the complainant and respondent, but also for their families, to ensure a holistic approach to resolving POSH issues and bringing down the reputational stigma that both parties have to face.

Techniques for Fair and Impartial Investigations

I have learned that ensuring fairness and impartiality in investigations is paramount but while investigating a case, I encountered a situation where bias was a significant concern. The complainant feared that the respondent's influential position would sway the IC members' investigation process. To address this issue some of the measures and several techniques that can be implemented to ensure a fair and impartial process as discussed below:

Key Points:

Establishing a Neutral Investigation Team: Forming a diverse investigation team from different departments helps eliminate potential biases. Including external members, such as myself, ensures neutrality and a different perspective on the investigation process.

Structured Interview Process: Using a standardized set of interview questions for all parties involved helps maintain consistency and fairness. Documenting interviews meticulously ensures not just accuracy but also transparency in the entire process.

Evidence-Based Approach: Basing conclusions solely on factual evidence and documented proof prevents personal biases from influencing the investigation. Cross-verifying evidence from multiple sources adds credibility to the findings where there is no scope for any bias to creep in.

Training and Awareness: Regular training sessions for IC members on recognizing and mitigating bias are indispensable. Developing a culture of continuous learning ensures that investigators are equipped to handle complex cases impartially and are not carried away by emotions.

Strategies for Handling Sensitive Cases with Minimal Distress

Handling sensitive cases requires a delicate balance of empathy and professionalism. In one particularly challenging case, as narrated by a POSH expert, the complainant was extremely distressed, fearing retaliation and the organization requested the External IC to implement strategies that minimized distress and provided support throughout the investigation. Some of the key points that can be implemented are discussed below:

Key Points:

Providing Safe Reporting Channels: Establishing anonymous and confidential reporting mechanisms encouraged individuals to come forward without fear. Regularly communicating these channels to employees fosters a sense of security.

Offering Psychological Support: Partnering with mental health professionals to provide counselling services to the complainant, respondent, and their families helps address emotional distress. Ensuring confidentiality in these sessions was crucial.

Minimizing Involvement of Unnecessary Parties: Limiting the number of individuals involved in the investigation preserves confidentiality and reduces anxiety for all parties. Keeping the circle small ensures that information is contained. Also, keeping the place of investigation in a closed private room will ensure not only confidentiality but also instil confidence in both parties.

Regular Updates and Reassurance: Regular updates on the progress of the investigation reassure the complainant and respondent that their concerns are being addressed. Maintaining open lines of communication is the key to reducing anxiety.

Maintaining Confidentiality and Nurturing Trust among Employees

Maintaining confidentiality is fundamental to nurturing trust within an organization. In one instance, a breach of confidentiality during an investigation led to widespread fear and mistrust among employees, in addition to legal penalties. This incident brought to light the importance of stringent measures to protect sensitive information.

Key Points:

Strict Confidentiality Agreements: Requiring all individuals involved in the investigation, including witnesses, to sign confidentiality agreements emphasizes the seriousness of maintaining discretion.

Secure Documentation and Storage: Implementing secure methods for storing investigation documents and evidence, such as encrypted digital storage, ensures that information is protected from unauthorized access.

Limited Disclosure: Sharing investigation details strictly on a need-to-know basis minimizes the risk of leaks. Even within the investigation team, limiting access to critical information is essential and should be permitted only when two IC members want to evaluate records on approval from the PO.

Building a Culture of Trust: Regularly communicating the organization's commitment to confidentiality and fair investigations fosters trust. Sharing the case outcomes and lessons learned anonymously reinforces this commitment at all levels of the organisation.

Psychological Safety for All Parties: Ensuring psychological support and counselling for both the complainant and respondent's families will help mitigate the broader emotional impact. Providing resources and support systems for affected families demonstrates a holistic approach to employee well-being. It also ensures that the complainant does not withdraw the case due to family pressure and reputational issues.

By adopting these techniques and strategies, organizations can address common concerns and fears associated with POSH investigations, ensuring fair, sensitive, and confidential handling of all cases. These approaches not only resolve immediate issues but also strengthen the overall trust and culture within the workplace.

Chapter 6:

Building a Supportive and Respectful Workplace

Building a Culture of Trust

As a POSH External Member in multiple organisations, I have witnessed the profound impact that a culture of trust, respect, and fairness can have on an organization. In one particular case, I was called in to help a company that had been struggling with recurring harassment issues despite having established policies and training programs. During my investigation, I realized that while the procedural aspects were in place, there was a significant gap in the organizational culture.

Reflecting on this experience, I understood that building a supportive and respectful workplace requires more than just compliance; it necessitates a deep cultural shift that prioritizes ongoing training, transparent communication, and a holistic approach to supporting all parties involved. In this section I make a humble attempt to suggest holistic solutions from my personal experiences and principles, emphasizing how these elements can create a thriving and respectful work environment.

Role of Ongoing Training and Transparent Communication

One of my most challenging cases involved a company where employees were reluctant to report harassment due to fear of retaliation and a lack of trust in the process. It was necessary for me to not only provide training to the employees but also intensive training to the IC members. The IC members' training ensured that they encouraged reporting sexual harassment, giving all the required support, and over a period of time, not only did employees feel heard, but even the instances of harassment came down to a very large extent. This highlighted the critical importance of ongoing training and transparent communication in fostering a safe and supportive workplace.

Key Points:

Regular Training Programs:

Continuous education for employees at all levels ensures that everyone is aware of POSH policies and their roles in maintaining a respectful workplace. Tailoring training to address specific organizational needs and scenarios enhances relevance and effectiveness.

Engaging and Interactive Sessions:

Incorporating role-plays, workshops, and real-life case studies into training sessions make them more engaging and impactful. Interactive sessions encourage participation and help employees better understand and retain the information.

Transparent Communication Channels:

Establishing open and transparent communication channels where employees feel safe to voice their concerns is crucial. Regular town halls, feedback sessions, and structured reporting mechanisms can help build trust and transparency.

Continuous Awareness Campaigns:

Implementing ongoing awareness campaigns using various media such as newsletters, posters, and digital platforms keeps POSH principles on top of mind for employees. Regular reminders reinforce the organization's commitment to a respectful workplace.

Implementing a Holistic Approach to Support All Parties Involved

During an investigation at a midsize firm, one of my friends working as an External IC encountered a situation in which both the complainant and the respondent were severely distressed, and the management was unsure how to handle the emotional fallout. This experience highlighted the need for a holistic approach that supports all parties involved.

Key Points:

Complainant Support:

Providing immediate psychological support and counselling to complainants helps them in navigating the emotional and mental stress associated with the investigation. Ensuring confidentiality and a safe environment for sharing their experiences is paramount.

Regular follow-ups and updates on the progress of the investigation reassure the complainant and respondent that their concerns are being taken seriously.

Respondent Support:

Offering counselling and support to respondents ensures they receive fair treatment and have the opportunity to share their side of the story, which fulfils the requirement of following principles of natural justice that is mandatory under the POSH Act. It's important to maintain neutrality and ensure the respondent's rights are protected throughout the process. This is especially important in scenarios of false sexual harassment complaints, which is nothing less than a character assassination and a severe reputation to the respondent. I have heard of a very disheartening instance where the respondent committed suicide due to reputational damage, and on completion of the investigation, it was found to be a false case. This instance outweighs the need for support to the respondent as well till truth surfaces on completion of the investigation process.

Clear communication about the investigation process and potential outcomes helps reduce anxiety and uncertainty for respondents.

Management Involvement:

The leadership and capability of the PO heading the POSH investigation effectively is crucial more so when it is a sensitive case. PO should be equipped to provide immediate support and maintain a balanced approach while dealing with such cases.

Ensuring a top-down approach of the management's active involvement in fostering a respectful workplace culture sets a strong example for employees to follow.

Continuous Improvement and Review of POSH Policies and Procedures

Creating a sustainable POSH framework requires regular reviews and continuous improvement to adapt to changing dynamics and ensure effectiveness. This was particularly evident in an organization where regular POSH audits and feedback led to significant enhancements in their POSH practices.

Key Points:

Recognizing and Rewarding Positive Behaviours:

Acknowledging and rewarding employees who exemplify respect and fairness reinforces positive behaviour. Recognition programs and awards for POSH champions can motivate others to follow suit.

Analysing POSH Incident Data:

Regular analysis of POSH incident data helps identify patterns and areas for improvement. Data-driven insights enable organizations to address root causes and prevent future incidents.

Regular Reviews and Audits by Leadership:

Conducting periodic reviews and audits of POSH policies and procedures by the leadership team ensures they remain relevant and effective. Engaging external experts for unbiased evaluations can provide valuable perspectives.

Integrating Personal Insights

Personal experiences and insights play a crucial role in shaping a supportive and respectful workplace. As a person involved in helping organisations with POSH issues, I have found that incorporating personal elements into the organizational culture can significantly enhance its effectiveness. Some of the key points I suggest for building a great work culture are:

Key Points:

Family Day:

Organizing family days and involving employees' families in workplace activities fosters a sense of community and support. It also reinforces the organization's commitment to a respectful and inclusive environment.

Team Building Activity:

Conducting regular team-building activities that promote collaboration, trust, and mutual respect strengthens workplace relationships. Activities that emphasize empathy and understanding can help break down barriers and build stronger teams.

Role of Leadership in Setting the Tone:

Leadership plays a pivotal role in setting the tone for a respectful workplace. Leaders must consistently demonstrate and uphold POSH principles, creating an environment where respect and fairness are non-negotiable.

Creating Peer Support Programs:

Establishing peer support programs or buddy programs where employees can mentor and support each other help in creating a network of trust and assistance. Peer support can be particularly effective in providing immediate help and guidance in sensitive situations.

By integrating these elements, organizations can build a supportive and respectful workplace that goes beyond compliance and fosters a culture of trust, respect, and fairness. This holistic approach ensures that POSH principles are not just policies on paper but are lived and practised daily, creating a thriving and safe work environment for all.

Frequently Asked Questions

Q1: How should we ensure confidentiality when receiving a complaint?

A1: Confidentiality should be maintained by ensuring the complaint is received in a secure environment, using confidential reporting channels such as a dedicated email or online portal with login credentials, and restricting access to the complaint details to only the IC members and necessary personnel.

Q2: What steps should we take if the witness wishes to remain anonymous?

A2: Anonymity of the witness can be respected by ensuring that the investigation focuses on the facts and evidence presented. IC should support the anonymity request of the witness and conduct the interview process in an outside location in a confidential manner.

Q3: How do we handle complaints received outside of formal channels?

A3: All complaints, regardless of how they are received, should be documented and treated with the same level of seriousness and monitoring. Encourage employees to use formal channels for proper documentation and follow-up.

Q4: What should we do if the complaint is vague or lacks details?

A4: Reach out to the complainant for additional information in the preliminary inquiry stage to understand the issue in-depth while assuring them of confidentiality. If they are reluctant, use the available details to start the preliminary inquiry and gather more information during the investigation.

Q5: How do we handle multiple complaints against the same respondent?

A5: Treat each complaint individually while looking for patterns or commonalities. Consolidate the investigations if they are related to the same incidents or behaviours to ensure a comprehensive approach.

Q6: What is the first step after receiving a complaint?

A6: Conduct a preliminary inquiry to determine if the complaint falls under the purview of the POSH Act. This involves reviewing the complaint, understanding the context, and deciding on the next steps.

Q7: How do we protect the complainant during the preliminary inquiry?

A7: Ensure the complainant's safety by keeping their identity confidential from other employees in the organisation, providing support and resources, and taking any necessary interim measures to prevent further harassment.

Q8: What if the preliminary inquiry reveals that the complaint is not related to sexual harassment?

A8: Document the findings and inform the complainant of the outcome. If the issue is related to other workplace concerns, refer it to the appropriate department or authority within the organization. As a further step, conduct POSH training for all employees, emphasising sexual and non-sexual behaviours.

Q9: What should the IC do if the Complainant is reluctant to complain as there is no evidence or witness to prove the allegation?

A9: The IC should assure the complainant that all complaints are taken seriously, that an investigation will be conducted based on the information provided, and that confidentiality and support will be maintained throughout the process. The IC should encourage the complainant to share all details they can, as evidence may still be uncovered during the investigation.

Q10: How long should the preliminary inquiry take?

A10: The preliminary inquiry should be conducted promptly, typically within a week, to decide whether a full investigation is warranted.

Q11: What are the key steps in conducting a POSH investigation?

A11: The key steps include:

- Preliminary inquiry of whether the complaint falls as defined in the POSH Act;

- Issuing 'Notice' to Complainant, Respondent, and Witnesses;
- Gathering and reviewing evidence;
- Conducting interviews with the complainant, respondent, and witnesses;
- Documenting all findings and maintaining confidentiality;
- Analysing the evidence to draw conclusions; and
- Drafting the report.

Q12: How do we ensure the investigation is fair and unbiased?

A12: Ensure impartiality by having a diverse investigation team, avoiding conflicts of interest, and basing conclusions solely on evidence. Provide training on unbiased investigation techniques to all IC members.

Q13: How do we handle uncooperative witnesses?

A13: Encourage cooperation by explaining the importance of their testimony and ensuring confidentiality. If witnesses remain uncooperative, document their reluctance and proceed with the available evidence.

Q14: What should be documented during the investigation?

A14: Document all interviews, evidence collected, decisions made, and the rationale behind those decisions. Ensure that all documentation is thorough, accurate, and securely stored.

Q15: How do we handle conflicting testimonies?

A15: Analyse all evidence and testimonies carefully, looking for corroborative evidence. If conflicts persist, consider the credibility and consistency of each testimony to draw conclusions.

Q16: What should be included in the investigation report?

A16: The investigation report should include:

- Summary of the complaint;
- Details of the investigation process;
- Evidence and testimonies collected;
- Findings and conclusions; and
- Recommendations for action.

Q17: How do we ensure the report is clear and comprehensive?

A17: Use clear and concise language, provide a logical flow of information, and ensure all key aspects of the investigation are covered. Review the report for completeness and accuracy before finalizing it.

Q18: Should the report include recommendations for disciplinary action?

A18: Yes, the report should include recommendations based on the findings. These recommendations should align with the organization's policies and the severity of the misconduct.

Q19: How do we protect the confidentiality of the individuals involved when drafting the report?

A19: Use anonymous identifiers such as, for example, C1 for Complainant and so on for all the parties involved, avoid sharing unnecessary details, and restrict access to the report to authorized personnel only.

Q20: What is the process for submitting and reviewing the investigation report?

A20: Submit the report to the relevant authorities within the organization, such as the HR department or senior management. Review the report in a confidential setting and ensure that all recommendations are considered and acted upon.

Q21: How do we communicate the investigation outcome to the complainant and respondent?

A21: Communicate the outcome confidentially and sensitively, providing a summary of the findings and the actions to be taken. Offer support and resources to both parties for presenting their opinions on the findings.

Q22: How to handle romantic relationships between employees in the organisation?

A22: Educate the employees on maintaining professional relationships with all employees in the organisation. Ensure to take a romantic relationship disclosure form from employees having a romantic relationship. The employees should also be instructed the employees to inform if there is any discord in the relationship in future to ensure their safety and cordial working relationship in the organisation. This process is absolutely essential if there is a reporting hierarchy between the two employees. Ensure that the actions are in line with the organization's policies during working hours.

Q23: How do we support the complainant post-investigation?

A23: Provide ongoing support and resources, such as counselling services and ensuring a safe work environment. Monitor the complainant's well-being and address any concerns they may have.

Q24: What if the complainant or respondent is not satisfied with the investigation outcome?

A24: Offer the complainant or the respondent an opportunity to appeal the decision through the organization's established appeal process. Ensure transparency and provide a clear explanation of the investigation process and reasoning for the findings.

Q25: How can we use the investigation findings to improve our POSH framework?

A25: Analyse the findings to identify patterns or gaps in the current POSH framework. Use these insights to update policies, enhance training programs, and implement measures to prevent future incidents.

Q26: How should we handle a complaint if the alleged incident occurred outside the workplace?

A26: The POSH Act covers incidents that occur anywhere work-related activities are conducted, including off-site events, client meetings, and business trips. Investigate the complaint as you would for any incident occurring within the workplace.

Q27: What if the complainant retracts their complaint?

A27: Document the retraction and understand the reasons behind it. Ensure that the complainant did not retract due to fear of retaliation or pressure. If there are indications of ongoing harassment, take necessary steps to provide interim relief, such as offering paid leave for a maximum period of three months or transferring the complainant or respondent to another department or location of the organisation. It is necessary for the IC to continue the investigation process and conclude it to ensure a safe workplace.

Q28: How do we address anonymous complaints?

A28: Investigate anonymous complaints based on the information provided. Treat anonymous complaints seriously. It is ideal in the organization's best interests to monitor the respondent (if the name is mentioned in the anonymous complaint) discreetly to ensure any unwanted behaviour does not continue.

Q29: How should we proceed if the complaint is made against a senior executive or management member?

A29: Ensure that the investigation is conducted impartially and without bias. Involve External IC member is necessary to avoid conflicts of interest. Maintain strict confidentiality and document all steps taken during the investigation. The role and responsibilities of IC members are independent and impartial, and hence, irrespective of the hierarchy of the respondents, it should be investigated. Maintain strict confidentiality and follow the same thorough investigation process as with any other complaint. If a need is felt by the IC committee, then the case can be reported to the Local Committee (LC).

Q30: How can we ensure that the complaint process is accessible to all employees?

A30: Provide multiple channels for reporting complaints, such as online portals, dedicated email addresses, and complaint boxes. Ensure that information about these channels is widely disseminated and easily accessible to all employees.

Q31: What role do External IC members play in POSH investigations?

A31: External IC member brings impartiality, expertise, and an unbiased perspective to the investigation. They can assist in conducting interviews, analysing evidence, and providing recommendations, especially in complex or high-stakes cases.

Q32: How do we handle evidence that is not directly related to the complaint?

A32: Document and review all evidence collected during the investigation. If evidence is not directly related to the complaint but indicates other issues, address it separately according to organizational policies.

Q33: What measures should be taken if the respondent retaliates against the complainant?

A33: Immediately address and investigate any retaliation claims. Take swift action to protect the complainant, such as implementing interim measures, and apply disciplinary actions against the respondent if retaliation is confirmed.

Q34: How do we manage conflicts of interest within the investigation team?

A34: Ensure that investigation team members have no personal or professional connections to the parties involved. If a conflict of interest arises, ask the IC member to recuse from the investigation process and reassign a new IC member to maintain impartiality.

Q35: How do we handle cases where both parties have conflicting information?

A35: Gather as much corroborative evidence as possible, including witness testimonies, documents, and digital evidence. Assess the credibility and consistency of all information and use a fact-based approach to draw conclusions.

Q36: What should be done if new information arises after the investigation is concluded?

A36: Reopen the investigation if the new information is significant and could impact the findings or conclusions. Document the new evidence and review the investigation process to ensure thoroughness and fairness.

Q37: How do we deal with non-cooperation from the respondent?

A37: Document the respondent's non-cooperation and proceed with the investigation based on available evidence. Inform the respondent of the potential consequences of non-cooperation and ensure that all efforts are made to gather their input.

Q38: How should we approach cases involving third-party harassment?

A38: Investigate third-party harassment cases with the same rigour as internal cases. Include third-party individuals in the investigation process, gather evidence, and take necessary actions to address the issue and prevent future incidents. If the issue is beyond the purview of the organization's IC committee, the complainant may be advised to report it to a nearby police station.

Q39: How detailed should the investigation report be?

A39: The report should be comprehensive and detailed, covering all aspects of the investigation, including the complaint summary, evidence collected, analysis, findings, and recommendations. Ensure clarity and conciseness to facilitate understanding.

Q40: What is the appropriate tone and language for the investigation report?

A40: Use professional, neutral, and objective language. Avoid any biased or emotional language and focus on presenting facts and evidence clearly and concisely.

Q41: How do we handle cases where the investigation findings are inconclusive?

A41: Document the findings and explain the reasons why they are inconclusive. Provide recommendations for preventive measures, further monitoring, or additional training to address potential issues and improve the workplace environment.

Q42: Should we include witness identities in the investigation report?

A42: Yes, it is necessary to include all the details of the witnesses' identities. But if there is a request from the witnesses to keep their identity anonymous then ensure to use anonymous identifiers in the report. Include sufficient information to understand their testimonies without compromising confidentiality.

Q43: How do we ensure that the investigation report is securely stored?

A43: Store the report in a secure, confidential location with restricted access. Use secure digital storage solutions and implement access controls to protect the report from unauthorized access.

Q44: How should we follow up with the complainant after the investigation?

A44: Provide the complainant with a summary of the findings and actions taken. Offer ongoing support, such as counselling services, and maintain regular check-ins to ensure their well-being and address any further concerns.

Q45: What steps should be taken to prevent retaliation against the complainant?

A45: Implement protective measures, such as monitoring the complainant's work environment, ensuring confidentiality, and taking swift action against any retaliation. Educate employees about anti-retaliation policies.

Q46: How do we reintegrate the respondent into the workplace if they are not found guilty?

A46: Communicate the investigation outcome to the respondent and provide support to reintegrate them into the workplace. Address any concerns or stigmas they may face and ensure a fair and respectful work environment.

Q47: What should be done if the complainant faces backlash from colleagues?

A47: Address any backlash immediately by reinforcing anti-retaliation policies and taking disciplinary actions against those responsible for the organisation's policies. Provide support and counselling to the complainant and foster a culture of respect and empathy.

Q48: How can we use investigation outcomes to improve workplace policies?

A48: Analyse the investigation outcomes to identify trends and gaps in existing policies. Use these insights to update and improve POSH policies, training programs, and preventive measures to create a safer workplace.

Q49: How do we ensure that the recommended actions are implemented effectively?

A49: Assign responsibility for implementing the recommended actions to specific individuals or departments assigning a timeline for implementation. Monitor the progress and effectiveness of these actions through regular follow-ups and evaluations.

Q50: What if an investigation report is leaked?

A50: Investigate the breach immediately, determine the source, and take appropriate disciplinary actions. Communicate transparently with the affected parties and implement stronger security measures to prevent future leaks.

Q51: How do we handle cases involving cross-border incidents?

A51: Follow the POSH Act guidelines while considering the laws and regulations of the involved countries. Collaborate with legal experts to ensure compliance and conduct a thorough and fair investigation.

Q52: What if the complaint is about an incident that occurred several years ago?

A52: Investigate the complaint based on the available evidence and testimonies. While older cases may present challenges, it is essential to address them to ensure justice and prevent future incidents.

Q53: How do we manage the stress and emotional toll on IC members during investigations?

A53: Provide IC members with access to counselling and support services. Ensure regular breaks and debriefing sessions to manage stress and prevent burnout. Foster a supportive environment within the IC.

Q54: How do we handle false complaints?

A54: Investigate all complaints thoroughly to determine their validity. If a complaint is found to be false, take appropriate disciplinary action against the complainant while ensuring that genuine complaints are still encouraged and taken seriously.

Q55: What if the complainant or respondent seeks legal action?

A55: The right to action is always with the Complainant, hence extending organisational cooperation with legal proceedings and providing all necessary documentation and evidence. Ensure that the investigation process complies with legal standards and seek legal counsel for guidance.

Q56: How do we balance the need for transparency with confidentiality?

A56: Maintain transparency in the investigation process and findings without disclosing confidential information. Provide general updates to employees about the investigation process and outcomes while protecting the identities of those involved.

Q57: How do we handle situations where the respondent is a valuable employee?

A57: Ensure impartiality and fairness regardless of the respondent's position or value to the organization. Base the investigation and subsequent actions solely on the facts and evidence. The respondent's unwelcome behaviour is more important than the value he adds to the organization, as ultimately, at some point, the organization's reputation is at huge risk and more valuable than anything else.

Q58: How can we ensure that temporary workers or contractors are aware of POSH policies?

A58: Include POSH training and policy briefings as part of the onboarding process for temporary workers and contractors. Ensure they have access to reporting channels and are aware of their rights and responsibilities.

Q59: How do we handle complaints involving cyber harassment?

A59: Investigate cyber harassment complaints by gathering digital evidence, such as emails, messages, and social media interactions. If available, work with IT and cyber security experts within the organisation to trace and document the harassment. Hiring external cyber experts on a need-basis if there is no internal cyber expert or team in the organisation to handle complaints can be a good step.

Q60: Can communication of the investigation process be done by any IC member?

A60: No, communication in the POSH investigation has to be done only by the PO. It is important to note that all meetings become null and void when conducted in the absence of the PO at any stage of the investigation process.

Q61: How do we encourage employees to come forward with complaints without fear of retaliation?

A61: Create a strong anti-retaliation policy, ensure confidentiality, and regularly communicate the importance of reporting. Offer multiple reporting channels and provide training to employees on their rights and protections under the POSH Act.

Q62: How do we handle complaints involving physical evidence, such as photographs or videos?

A62: Collect, preserve, and document all physical evidence in a secure and confidential manner. Limit access and use proper storage methods to ensure the integrity of the evidence. Include the evidence in the investigation report while maintaining confidentiality.

Q63: How should we address cultural differences that may influence perceptions of harassment?

A63: Be culturally sensitive and aware during investigations. Provide training to IC members on cultural differences and how they may impact perceptions of behaviour. Ensure that the investigation is conducted impartially and based on the facts and evidence.

Q64: How do we ensure that the investigation process is trauma-informed?

A64: Provide training to IC members on trauma-informed investigation techniques. Approach complainants with empathy, avoid re-traumatizing them during interviews and offer access to counselling and support services throughout the investigation process.

Q65: How should we handle complaints made by third parties or witnesses?

A65: Investigate third-party or witness complaints with the same rigour as direct complaints, even though only the complainant should make a formal complaint as per the Act. Gather evidence and testimonies from all relevant parties and ensure confidentiality throughout the process. It is important to report to the authorised authorities within and outside the organisation (police) as necessary to control future issues.

Q66: How do we deal with counter-complaints made by the respondent?

A66: Investigate counter-complaints separately but concurrently, ensuring impartiality and fairness to both parties. Document all findings and maintain confidentiality for both the original complaint and the counter-complaint.

Q67: How should we approach cases involving consensual relationships that are now claimed as harassment?

A67: Investigate the complaint by gathering evidence and testimonies to understand the context and dynamics of the relationship. Assess whether any power imbalances or coercion were involved and base conclusions on the facts and evidence.

Q68: How do we handle complaints involving non-verbal harassment, such as gestures or body language?

A68: Investigate non-verbal harassment complaints by gathering testimonies from the complainant, witnesses, and respondent. Consider the context, frequency, and impact of the behaviour. Document findings and include them in the investigation report.

Q69: What should we do if the complainant or respondent refuses to participate in the investigation?

A69: Document the refusal and proceed with the investigation based on available evidence to reach a conclusion. Inform both parties of the potential impact of non-participation on the investigation's outcome.

Q70: How do we ensure the safety of the investigation team when handling high-risk cases?

A70: Implement safety measures such as conducting interviews in secure locations, using secure communication channels, and involving security personnel if necessary. Ensure that all IC members are aware of and follow safety protocols.

Q71: How do we address discrepancies in witness testimonies in the investigation report?

A71: Document all witness testimonies accurately, noting any discrepancies. Analyse the credibility and consistency of each testimony and provide a rationale for the conclusions drawn. Include a summary of how discrepancies were addressed in the report.

Q72: How should we handle cases where the evidence is primarily available only in digital mode?

A72: Securely collect, preserve, and document digital evidence, such as emails, messages, and social media posts. Work with IT and cyber security experts to ensure the integrity of the evidence, as morphing is a possibility. Include digital evidence in the investigation report while maintaining confidentiality.

Q73: How do we ensure that the investigation report aligns with legal requirements?

A73: Ensure that the investigation report complies with the POSH Act and any other relevant legal requirements. Seek assistance from external IC members to review the report and provide guidance on legal compliance.

Q74: What can be done if the IC is unable to complete the investigation within the stipulated 90-day period?

A74: The IC can record valid reasons for the delay in completing the investigation process. The IC can extend the process for a further 90 days.

Q75: How should we approach cases where the complainant or respondent quits the organization during the investigation?

A75: Continue the investigation to its conclusion regardless of the complainant or respondent's departure. Document all findings and take appropriate action based on the evidence. Ensure that the organization's policies and procedures are followed.

Q76: How do we use the outcomes of POSH investigations to improve organizational culture?

A76: Analyse the outcomes of POSH investigations to identify trends and areas for improvement. Use these insights to update policies, enhance training programs, and implement preventive measures. Foster a culture of respect and safety by continuously reinforcing positive behaviours and addressing issues promptly.

Q77: How do we ensure that employees are aware of the support available to them during and after an investigation?

A77: Communicate regularly about the support services available, such as counselling and assistance of the IC members. Provide information during training sessions, on the company intranet, and through other internal communication channels. Ensure that employees know how to access these services.

Q78: What should IC do if the Complainant is reluctant to complain because her co-worker is advising her to do so? Should IC take disciplinary action against the co-worker for discouraging the Complainant from filing her complaint?

A78: The IC should first speak with the complainant to understand the reasons behind the co-worker's advice and ensure the complainant feels supported in coming forward. The IC should then address the co-worker's behavior through appropriate channels, emphasizing the importance of supporting individuals in reporting harassment, but disciplinary action should only be considered if it is clear that the co-worker's advice was meant to obstruct the complaint process or intimidate the complainant.

Q79: How can we ensure that the learnings from POSH investigations are integrated into future training programs?

A79: Review the outcomes and findings from POSH investigations regularly and update training programs accordingly. Incorporate real-life scenarios, lessons learned, and best practices into training sessions to enhance understanding and preparedness.

Q80: How do we handle complaints involving multiple respondents?

A80: Investigate each respondent's involvement individually while looking for patterns or commonalities. Ensure that the investigation process is fair, thorough, and impartial for all parties involved. Document findings and take appropriate actions based on the evidence.

Q81: What should we do if the respondent goes absconding during the investigation process?

A81: Document the entire investigation process and depending on the severity of the sexual harassment steps should be taken to file a complaint with the police. This is important to ensure the safety of the complainant and bring the respondent to the doors of justice in order to ensure faith is reinstated not just for the complainant but all employees in the organisation.

Q82: How do we address concerns about bias in the investigation process?

A82: Ensure transparency in the investigation process, involve diverse and impartial investigation team members, and involving external IC which is mandatory as per the Act. Document all steps taken and provide clear, evidence-based findings to address concerns about bias.

Q83: How should we manage the potential impact of high-profile cases on organizational reputation?

A83: Handle high-profile cases with utmost confidentiality and professionalism. Communicate transparently with stakeholders while protecting the identities of those involved. Take swift and appropriate actions based on the investigation findings to demonstrate the organisation's commitment to a safe and respectful workplace.

Q84: Can IC take suo moto cognizance of a sexual harassment case if there is an anonymous complaint?

A84: The Posh Act does not allow IC to take Suo moto cognizance of a sexual harassment case by an anonymous complainant. However, the primary role of IC in an organisation is not only to address sexual harassment cases but also to prevent their occurrence through proactive measures. Thus, the IC can speak with the respondent on the anonymous complaint received and brief about the policies of the company. IC can advise the respondent that sexual harassment will not be tolerated and strict measures will be initiated if allegations are proven. Also, inform the respondent of his being put under observation for any misconduct.

Q85: What can the IC do if the complainant insists that she wants to file a police report?

A85: The IC committee should investigate the complaint for gravity and provide all necessary support to the complainant so that she can file a case with the police. IC members should note that, as per section 19(g), the employer should aid the woman if she wishes to file a complaint with the police.

Q86: How do we ensure that the complainant and respondent are not in contact during the investigation?

A86: Implement measures such as changing work schedules, reassigning duties, or providing temporary remote work options. This is very important in scenarios where there is a reporting relationship between the complainant and the respondent. Communicate clearly with both parties about the need for separation and ensure that these measures do not appear punitive.

Q87: How do we handle cases involving employees from different locations or departments?

A87: Coordinate with relevant departments and locations to gather evidence and conduct interviews. Ensure that the investigation team understands the organizational structure and context. Maintain clear communication and confidentiality across all locations.

Q88: How should we approach cases where the alleged harassment occurred outside of the workplace?

A88: Investigate incidents that occur outside the workplace if they have a direct impact on the work environment or involve colleagues. Gather evidence and testimonies and assess the context and impact on the workplace. Document findings and take appropriate actions as necessary, such as helping the complainant file a police complaint.

Q89: Can the complainant be granted leave during the investigation process if requested by the complainant? What can IC do if the complainant seeks an extension of leave beyond the stipulated three months?

A89: As per section 12(1)(b) of the POSH Act, the complainant should be provided with interim relief, which includes granting paid leave for three months. The IC committee needs to take a few things into account before granting leave beyond the stipulated three months. Firstly, IC can grant leave beyond the stipulated period if the investigation process and the final decision have not been completed within three months. Secondly, if there is any physical or mental disability on the production of a medical certificate, an extension of leave can be granted to the complainant.

Q90: How do we handle complaints that involve external parties, such as clients or vendors?

A90: Investigate the complaint with the same rigour as internal cases. Communicate with the external parties involved, gather evidence, and document findings. Address the issue through appropriate channels, such as contract management or legal action, if necessary. Also, report the matter to the external parties' employers to ensure investigation at their end.

Q91: How do we ensure that the investigation report is easily understandable?

A91: Use clear and concise language, avoid legal jargon, and structure the report logically. Include an executive summary, key findings, and conclusions. Ensure that the report is accessible to all relevant stakeholders while maintaining confidentiality.

Q92: What should we include in the recommendations section of the investigation report?

A92: Based on the findings, provide specific, actionable recommendations. Include measures to address the complaint, prevent future incidents, and improve workplace culture. Ensure that recommendations are practical, realistic, and aligned with organizational policies.

Q93: How do we handle the reintegration of the complainant and respondent after the investigation?

A93: Develop a reintegration plan that addresses the needs of both parties. Provide support services such as counselling, mediation, or conflict resolution. Communicate clearly with both parties about the steps taken and ensure that the reintegration process is respectful and fair.

Q94: How do we measure the effectiveness of our POSH policies and procedures?

A94: Conduct regular reviews and audits of POSH policies and procedures. Gather feedback from employees, monitor the number and nature of complaints, and assess the outcomes of investigations. Use these insights to continuously improve and update policies. Involve an external IC member to review company policies to identify any gaps and address them properly.

Q95: How should we handle cases where both the complainant and respondent are valuable employees?

A95: Conduct the investigation impartially and based on the evidence. Ensure that the process is fair and respectful to both parties. Address the findings appropriately and take actions that are consistent with organizational policies and the principles of justice and fairness. An important factor to consider is the organisation's values in ensuring a safe workplace rather than ignoring the inappropriate behaviours of either of the parties involved, no matter how valuable they are for the organisation.

Q96: How do we handle complaints involving bullying or intimidation tactics?

A96: Investigate bullying and intimidation complaints with the same rigour as sexual harassment complaints. Gather evidence from the complainant, respondent, and witnesses. Document findings and take appropriate actions to address the behaviour and prevent recurrence. This investigation can be undertaken by the senior HR team and need not be by the IC members in the organisation. Ensure that all policies are in place for handling any unwelcome behaviour.

Q97: What should we do if the complaint is related to a previous incident that was not reported at that point in time?

A97: Investigate the complaint even if the incident occurred in the past. Collect available evidence and testimonies, and assess the context and impact of the delay in reporting. Document findings and take appropriate actions based on the evidence if harassment is found.

Q98: How can we ensure that our investigation process respects the privacy of both the complainant and the respondent?

A98: Implement strict confidentiality measures throughout the investigation process which is also the mandate as per the POSH Act. Limit access to information to only those directly involved in the investigation. Use secure communication channels and document all steps taken to protect privacy.

Q99: How should we handle complaints that are based on misunderstandings or miscommunication?

A99: Investigate the complaint thoroughly to understand the context and details of the misunderstanding. Gather evidence and testimonies from all parties involved to understand the gravity of misunderstandings or miscommunication. Provide recommendations to address communication issues and prevent future misunderstandings.

Q100: What steps can we take to support employees during a prolonged investigation?

A100: Provide regular updates to both the complainant and respondent about the investigation's progress. Offer access to counselling and support services to help them cope with the stress. Ensure that their work environment remains respectful and free from retaliation during the investigation.

Sample Templates, Notices and Checklist

POSH Complaint Form
Template

[Company Name] POSH Complaint Form

This form is designed to facilitate the reporting of incidents of sexual harassment as defined under the POSH Act, 2013. All information provided will be kept confidential.

1. Complainant Information

- **Name:**

- **Employee ID:**

- **Department:**

- **Position:**

- **Contact Number:**

- **Email Address:**

- **Preferred method of communication (phone/email/in-person):**

2. Incident Details

- **Date of Incident:**

- **Time of Incident:**

- **Location of Incident:**

3. Details of the Person(s) Involved

- **Name of Respondent(s):**

- **Position/Title of Respondent(s):**

- **Department of Respondent(s):**

- *Relationship to Complainant (e.g., colleague, supervisor, client):*

4. Witnesses (if any)

- *Name(s) of Witness(es):*

- *Position/Title of Witness(es):*

- *Contact Information of Witness(es):*

5. Description of the Incident

Please provide a detailed description of the incident, including any verbal or physical actions, gestures, or behaviours that you believe constitute sexual harassment.

6. Supporting Evidence (if any)

Please list and attach any documents, emails, messages, or other evidence that support your complaint.

7. Actions Taken (if any)

- **Have you taken any action or reported this incident to anyone prior to this? If yes, please provide details:**

8. Desired Outcome

Please specify the action you wish the Internal Committee to take:

Declaration

- *I, [Complainant's Name], hereby declare that the information provided in this complaint form is true and accurate to the best of my knowledge and belief. I understand that any false statements or omissions may result in disciplinary action or may affect the outcome of the investigation.*

- *I shall abide by the confidentiality of such proceedings. That I shall not disclose such information jeopardizing the proceedings with any person, unless mandated so or expressly permitted by the authority of law.*

- *I fully understand that in the event of any direct or indirect breach of the confidentiality, the organisation has right to construe such breach as a gross violation of law and organisation policy and I shall be liable for disciplinary action or any other action in accordance with law.*

- *I hereby declare that this my name and signature and what is stated above is true and that I will fully cooperate with the investigation process.*

Signature of Complainant:

Date:

For Internal Committee Use Only

- **Received By (Name):**

- *Date Received:*

- *Case Reference Number:*

- *Initial Review Date:*

- *Assigned IC Member(s):*

Confidentiality Statement

All information provided in this form will be treated with the utmost confidentiality and will only be disclosed to those directly involved in the investigation process.

This form is intended to ensure a safe and respectful workplace. Your courage in reporting this incident is appreciated and will contribute to a positive and safe working environment.

[Company Name]

[Company Address]

[Contact Information for POSH Committee]

POSH Investigation: Complainant Notice Template

To,

[Insert employee's name]

[Insert designation]

[Insert place of posting]

Subject: Notice to appear before the POSH Internal Committee

Mam,

Your complaint was received by the Internal Committee on __________ [insert date]. Kindly acknowledge receipt of the notice. You are required to appear before the committee on _________ [insert date] at __________ [insert time] at _________ [address of the place of meeting] along with relevant documents, evidence, and the list of witnesses, if any.

Please note that you should attend the meeting personally. No third party (including a legal practitioner) can represent the Complainant.

(Signed by Chairperson of IC)

(Name & designation)

POSH Investigation: Respondent Notice Template

To,

[Insert employee's name]

[Insert designation]

[Insert place of posting]

Subject: Notice to appear before the POSH Internal Committee

Sir,

This is to bring to your notice, that a complaint has been filed against you by [Insert name of the complainant] with the Internal Committee on Sexual Harassment on [Insert date].

Please refer to the attached copy of the sexual harassment complaint received by the committee on [insert date].

Kindly acknowledge receipt of the notice. You are required to appear before the committee on _________ [insert date] at _________ [insert time] at _________ [address of the place of meeting] along with relevant documents, evidence, and the list of witnesses, if any, within 10 days of receipt of this notice.

Please note that you should attend the meeting personally. The respondent cannot be represented by a third party (including a legal practitioner).

(Signed by Chairperson of IC)

(Name & designation)

POSH Investigation: Complainant Interview Template

[Company Name]

POSH Investigation: Complainant Interview

Interview Details:

- *Date:*

- *Time:*

- *Location:*

- *Interviewer(s):*

Complainant Information:

- *Name:*

- *Employee ID:*

- *Department:*

- *Position:*

- *Contact Number:*

- *Email Address:*

1. Background Information:

- *Can you please provide a brief overview of your role and responsibilities within the company?*

- *How long have you been working with our organization?*

- Can you describe your working relationship with the respondent prior to the incident?

- How often did you interact with the respondent before the incident?

- Have there been any previous disagreements or conflicts between you and the respondent?

- How would you describe your overall work experience at the company prior to this incident?

2. Incident Details:

- Can you describe the incident(s) in detail?

- When did the incident(s) occur (date and time)?

- Where did the incident(s) take place?

- Were there any witnesses to the incident(s)? If so, who were they?

- What was the atmosphere like at the time of the incident?

- Were there any immediate reactions from others present during the incident?

- Did you take any notes or document the incident immediately after it occurred?

3. Nature of the Harassment:

- *What specific actions or behaviours did the respondent engage in that you found inappropriate or offensive?*

- *Was there any physical contact involved? If so, please describe.*

- *Did the respondent make any verbal comments or remarks? If so, what were they?*

- *Were there any gestures or body language that made you feel uncomfortable?*

- *Did the respondent use any digital communication (emails, texts, social media) to harass you?*

- *Were there any prior warnings or indications that the respondent might behave in this manner?*

- *How did the respondent react when you expressed discomfort or asked them to stop?*

4. Context and Repetition:

- *Was this an isolated incident or part of a pattern of behaviour?*

- *If it was repeated, how many times did similar incidents occur?*

- *Did you notice any change in the respondent's behaviour over time?*

- *Have you observed the respondent engaging in similar behaviour with others?*

- *Did the intensity or frequency of the behaviour increase over time?*

- *Were there any specific triggers or circumstances that seemed to prompt the respondent's behaviour?*

5. Impact on You:

- *How did the incident(s) affect you personally and professionally?*

- *Did the incident(s) impact your ability to perform your job duties?*

- *Have you experienced any emotional or psychological effects as a result of the incident(s)?*

- *Did the incident(s) affect your relationships with colleagues or supervisors?*

- *Have you experienced any physical symptoms related to stress or anxiety from the incident(s)?*

- *Have you had to take time off work or seek medical attention because of the incident(s)?*

6. Response and Action Taken:

- *How did you respond to the respondent during and after the incident?*

- *Did you inform anyone about the incident immediately after it occurred? If yes, whom did you inform and what was their response?*

- Have you taken any steps to avoid the respondent since the incident?

- Did you document your response to the incident(s) in any way?

- Have you sought advice or support from any external organizations or authorities?

- Did you receive any follow-up or feedback after reporting the incident?

7. Prior Incidents:

- Have you experienced any similar incidents in the past with the same respondent or anyone else within the organization?

- If yes, did you report those incidents? If so, what was the outcome?

- How do these previous incidents compare to the current one?

- Have you heard of similar complaints about the respondent from other colleagues?

- Did you notice any changes in the respondent's behaviour after previous incidents were reported?

- Were any preventive measures or actions taken by the company after previous incidents?

8. Support and Assistance:

- *Have you sought any support or assistance (e.g., counselling, medical help) after the incident?*

- *Are you aware of the resources and support systems available within the organization for such matters?*

- *Have you discussed the incident with friends or family members?*

- *Do you feel you have received adequate support from the company's HR or management?*

- *Have you attended any company training or workshops on sexual harassment and support resources?*

- *Would additional support or resources from the company be helpful to you?*

9. Evidence and Documentation:

- *Do you have any documents, emails, messages, or other forms of evidence that support your complaint?*

- *Are there any other witnesses who can corroborate your account of the incident?*

- *Have you preserved any physical evidence (e.g., clothing, items involved in the incident)?*

- *Have you taken any photographs or screenshots related to the incident?*

- *Did you keep a journal or record of the incidents and your responses?*

- Can you provide a timeline or sequence of events that highlights key moments of the harassment?

10. Desired Outcome:

- What outcome are you seeking from this investigation?

- Do you have any specific requests or recommendations for how this matter should be resolved?

- What steps would make you feel safer and more comfortable at work?

- Are you seeking any specific disciplinary action against the respondent?

- Would you like to see any changes in company policy or procedures as a result of this incident?

- Is there any way the company can support your professional growth and well-being after the incident?

11. Understanding of the Process:

- Are you aware of the procedures involved in the POSH investigation?

- Do you have any questions or concerns about the investigation process?

- Have you received any written or verbal communication about the investigation process from the company?

- *Are you familiar with your rights under the POSH Act, 2013?*

- *Do you understand the potential outcomes of the investigation?*

- *Is there anything specific about the process that you find unclear or concerning?*

12. Confidentiality and Retaliation:

- *Are you concerned about confidentiality and the protection of your identity during this investigation?*

- *Have you experienced or are you worried about any form of retaliation since reporting the incident?*

- *Have you noticed any changes in your work environment or treatment by colleagues since the incident?*

- *Do you feel confident that the company will protect your privacy during the investigation?*

- *Have you experienced any threats or intimidation related to your complaint?*

- *What measures do you think the company should take to ensure your safety and confidentiality?*

13. Other Relevant Information:

- *Is there any other information or details you would like to share that you believe are relevant to this investigation?*

- Are there any additional witnesses or evidence that you think we should consider?

- Have you had any follow-up interactions with the respondent since the incident?

- Are there any specific dates or events that you believe are crucial to understanding the incident?

- Have you received any communication from the respondent since the incident?

- Do you have any suggestions for improving the investigation process?

14. Clarification and Follow-Up:

- Do you need any clarification about the questions asked or the investigation process?

- How would you like to be updated on the progress of the investigation?

- Would you prefer regular updates via email, phone, or in-person meetings?

- Do you have any concerns about the duration or timeline of the investigation?

- Is there a specific person in the company you would prefer to be your point of contact?

- Are there any specific follow-up actions you would like the company to take?

15. Final Comments:

- Do you have any final comments or concerns you would like to address?

- Is there anything we haven't covered that you feel is important to mention?

- Do you have any questions for the investigation team?

- Are there any additional resources or support you would like to request from the company?

- How do you feel about the overall approach and tone of this interview?

- Is there anything else you would like to share about your experience or expectations?

16. Work Environment:

- How would you describe the general work environment and culture in your department?

- Do you believe the incident was influenced by any cultural or environmental factors in the workplace?

- How have your colleagues and supervisors responded to the incident?

- Are there any specific aspects of the work environment that you believe contribute to the issue?

- *Have there been any recent changes in the workplace culture or management that might be relevant?*

- *Do you feel that there is an open and supportive atmosphere for reporting such incidents?*

17. Respondent's Behaviour:

- *Prior to the incident, did you notice any behaviour from the respondent that you found concerning?*

- *How would you describe your interactions with the respondent before the incident?*

- *Did the respondent display similar behaviour towards others in the workplace?*

- *Have you ever confronted the respondent about their behaviour? If so, what was their response?*

- *Did you observe any changes in the respondent's behaviour after the incident?*

- *Have other colleagues mentioned similar concerns about the respondent to you?*

18. Witness Accounts:

- *Have you spoken to any witnesses about the incident? If so, what did they say?*

- *Are there any witnesses you believe are reluctant to come forward?*

- Do you think the witnesses would be willing to provide a statement or testify?

- How did the witnesses react during and after the incident?

- Have you observed any changes in the behaviour or attitude of the witnesses since the incident?

- Do you have any suggestions for how we can encourage witnesses to come forward?

19. Timeline:

- Can you provide a timeline of events leading up to the incident?

- What happened immediately after the incident?

- Are there any key dates or periods that are particularly relevant to the investigation?

- Did the respondent's behaviour change over the course of your interactions?

- Have there been any significant events or changes in the workplace since the incident?

- Can you identify any specific moments that escalated the situation?

20. Response from Management:

- *How do you feel the management has handled your complaint so far?*

- *Do you feel supported by your supervisors or HR in this matter?*

- *Have you received any feedback or follow-up from management since reporting the incident?*

- *Do you believe management has taken your complaint seriously?*

- *Are there any actions or responses from management that you found particularly helpful or unhelpful?*

- *How would you like management to address your concerns moving forward?*

21. Workplace Policies:

- *Are you familiar with the company's policies on sexual harassment?*

- *Do you feel these policies are adequately enforced?*

- *Have you received any training or information on the company's sexual harassment policies?*

- *Do you think the current policies are effective in preventing and addressing harassment?*

- *Are there any gaps or areas of improvement you would suggest for the policies?*

- *How would you rate the company's overall approach to handling sexual harassment complaints?*

22. Suggestions for Improvement:

- *Do you have any suggestions on how the company can improve its handling of sexual harassment cases?*

- *Are there any specific changes you would like to see in the workplace environment or policies?*

- *How can the company better support employees who report harassment?*

- *What additional resources or training do you think would be helpful?*

- *Are there any best practices from other organizations that you think the company should adopt?*

- *How can the company ensure a more respectful and inclusive workplace culture?*

23. Emotional and Mental Health:

- *Have you sought any professional help for emotional or mental health issues related to the incident?*

- *Do you feel the need for any specific support from the company?*

- *How has the incident affected your mental health and well-being?*

- *Have you experienced any ongoing stress or anxiety as a result of the incident?*

- *Are there any coping strategies or support systems that have been helpful to you?*

- *Would you like to request any accommodations or adjustments at work to support your mental health?*

24. Past Incidents:

- *Have you faced similar incidents in your previous workplaces? If so, how were they handled?*

- *How does this incident compare to past experiences?*

- *Were there any lessons learned from previous incidents that could apply to this situation?*

- *Have you discussed your past experiences with anyone at the company?*

- *Do you believe your past experiences have influenced how you handled the current incident?*

- *Are there any patterns or similarities between this incident and previous ones?*

25. Personal Reflection:

- *How do you feel about continuing to work in the same environment?*

- *What would make you feel safer and more comfortable at work moving forward?*

- *How has this experience impacted your view of the company?*

- *Are there any long-term changes you would like to see in the workplace culture?*

- *Do you have any personal goals or actions you plan to take as a result of this experience?*

- *How can the company support your career growth and well-being after the incident?*

Signature of Complainant:

Date:

Interviewer's Notes:

- **Summary of the Complainant's Statements:**

- **Observations:**

- **Next Steps:**

Confidentiality Statement

All information provided in this interview will be treated with the utmost confidentiality and will only be disclosed to those directly involved in the investigation process.

[Company Name]

[Company Address]

[Contact Information for POSH Committee]

POSH Investigation: Respondent Interview Template

[Company Name]

POSH Investigation: Respondent Interview

Interview Details:

- *Date:*

- *Time:*

- *Location:*

- *Interviewer(s):*

Respondent Information:

- *Name:*

- *Employee ID:*

- *Department:*

- **Position:**

- **Contact Number:**

- **Email Address:**

Introduction

- **Introduction to the Interview: Explain the purpose of the interview, confidentiality, and the importance of honesty.**

- **Explanation of Rights: Inform the respondent of their rights, including the right to be heard, the right to confidentiality, and the right to a fair investigation.**

- **Overview of the Process: Provide an overview of the investigation process and what will happen next.**

Basic Information

1. **Personal Information:**

   - Can you please confirm your full name and current position in the organization?

   - How long have you been employed with our organization?

   - What are your current job responsibilities?

2. **Understanding of the Complaint:**

   - Are you aware of the complaint that has been made against you?

o   Can you summarize your understanding of the
    allegations?

Contextual Questions

3. **Work Relationship:**

    o   What is your working relationship with the
        complainant?

    o   How frequently do you interact with the
        complainant in a professional setting?

4. **Interaction Details:**

    o   Can you describe the nature of your interactions
        with the complainant?

    o   Have there been any recent changes in your
        interactions or working relationship with the
        complainant?

Incident-Specific Questions

5. **Incident Description:**

    o   Can you describe in detail your version of the
        incident(s) mentioned in the complaint?

    o   Where and when did these incidents allegedly
        occur?

6. **Witnesses:**

- o   *Were there any witnesses present during the incident(s)?*

- o   *Can you provide the names of any individuals who might have witnessed the interactions?*

7. **Communications:**

- o   *Have you had any email, text, or other written communications with the complainant? If so, can you provide details or copies?*

Behaviour and Intent

8. **Perception of Actions:**

- o   *How do you perceive your actions during the incident(s)?*

- o   *Did you intend for your actions to be interpreted in the manner described by the complainant?*

9. **Prior Incidents:**

- o   *Have you had any prior incidents or complaints of this nature against you?*

- o   *How were those incidents resolved?*

10. **Motivations:**

- o   *Can you provide any context or motivations behind your actions during the incident(s)?*

- o   Were there any external factors influencing your behaviours?

Response and Impact

11. **Response to Allegations:**

    - o   What is your response to the specific allegations made against you?

    - o   Do you have any evidence or documentation to support your version of events?

12. **Impact on Work:**

    - o   How has the complaint and investigation process impacted your work and professional relationships?

    - o   Have you experienced any changes in your work environment since the complaint was filed?

Reflective Questions

13. **Self-Reflection:**

    - o   In retrospect, is there anything you would have done differently in your interactions with the complainant?

    - o   How do you feel about the current situation and the allegations against you?

14. **Learning and Improvement:**

- What steps do you think could be taken to prevent similar incidents in the future?

- Are there any training or resources you believe would be beneficial for improving workplace interactions?

Additional Questions

15. **Support Systems:**

    - Have you sought support or advice from anyone within or outside the organization regarding the complaint?

    - How can the organization support you during this investigation process?

16. **Clarification and Context:**

    - Are there any additional details or context you would like to provide regarding the incident(s)?

    - Is there anything else you believe the investigation committee should know?

17. **Workplace Culture:**

    - How would you describe the current workplace culture in your department?

    - Do you feel there are any underlying issues or tensions that may have contributed to the complaint?

18. Feedback on Process:

- o How has your experience been with the investigation process so far?

- o Do you have any feedback on how the process could be improved?

19. Witnesses:

- o Are there any individuals you believe the investigation committee should speak with to gain a better understanding of the situation?

- o Can you provide their contact information?

20. Mitigating Factors:

- o Are there any mitigating factors or circumstances that you believe should be considered in the investigation?

- o How do you think these factors might influence the outcome?

21. Future Steps:

- o What steps do you plan to take moving forward, regardless of the investigation's outcome?

- o How do you intend to address the situation with the complainant and your colleagues?

22. Awareness of Policies:

- o Are you aware of the organization's POSH policies and guidelines?

- o Have you received any training on these policies? If so, when?

23. Resolution Preferences:

- o What would be your preferred resolution to this situation?

- o How do you believe the organization can facilitate a fair and just outcome?

24. Relationship with Complainant:

- o Have you had any prior conflicts or issues with the complainant before this incident?

- o How would you describe your overall relationship with the complainant over time?

25. Additional Comments:

- o Is there anything else you would like to add that has not been covered in this interview?

- o Do you have any questions about the investigation process or next steps?

Signature of Respondent:

Date:

Interviewer's Notes:

- *Summary of the Respondent's Statements:*

- *Observations:*

- *Next Steps:*

Confidentiality Statement

All information provided in this interview will be treated with the utmost confidentiality and will only be disclosed to those directly involved in the investigation process.

[Company Name]

[Company Address]

[Contact Information for POSH Committee]

POSH Investigation: Witness Interview Template

[Company Name]

POSH Investigation: Witness Interview

Interview Details:

- *Date:*

- *Time:*

- *Location:*

- *Interviewer(s):*

Witness Information:

- *Name:*

- *Employee ID:*

- *Department:*

- *Position:*

- *Contact Number:*

- *Email Address:*

Introduction

- *Introduction to the Interview: Explain the purpose of the interview, confidentiality, and the importance of honesty.*

- *Explanation of Rights: Inform the witness of their rights, including the right to confidentiality and the importance of impartiality.*

- *Overview of the Process: Provide an overview of the investigation process and what will happen next.*

Basic Information

1. *Personal Information:*

o   Can you please confirm your full name and current position in the organization?

o   How long have you been employed with our organization?

o   What are your current job responsibilities?

2. **Understanding of the Complaint:**

o   Are you aware of the complaint that has been made?

o   How did you become aware of the complaint?

Contextual Questions

3. **Work Relationship:**

o   What is your working relationship with the complainant and the respondent?

o   How frequently do you interact with the complainant and the respondent in a professional setting?

4. **Interaction Details:**

o   Can you describe the nature of your interactions with both the complainant and the respondent?

o   Have there been any recent changes in your interactions or working relationship with either party?

Incident-Specific Questions

5. **Incident Observation:**

   o   *Were you present during the incident(s) mentioned in the complaint?*

   o   *Can you describe in detail what you observed during the incident(s)?*

6. **Incident Details:**

   o   *Where and when did the incident(s) occur?*

   o   *Were there any other individuals present during the incident(s)?*

7. **Behaviour Observation:**

   o   *How did the complainant and respondent behave during the incident(s)?*

   o   *Did you notice any verbal or non-verbal cues that stood out to you?*

Communication and Evidence

8. **Communications:**

   o   *Have you had any communications (emails, texts, etc.) with the complainant or respondent regarding the incident(s)?*

   o   *Can you provide details or copies of these communications?*

9. **Evidence:**

- o Do you have any physical evidence (documents, photos, etc.) related to the incident(s)?

- o Can you share this evidence with the investigation committee?

10. **Additional Observations:**

- o Did you observe any interactions between the complainant and respondent outside of the incident(s)?

- o Can you describe these interactions and their context?

Perception and Impact

11. **Perception of Actions:**

- o How do you perceive the actions of the complainant and respondent during the incident(s)?

- o Did you find any behaviour particularly concerning or noteworthy?

12. **Impact on Work:**

- o How has the incident and subsequent complaint impacted the work environment?

- o *Have you noticed any changes in the behaviour or performance of the complainant or respondent since the incident?*

Reflective Questions

13. **Workplace Culture:**

    - o *How would you describe the current workplace culture in your department?*

    - o *Do you feel there are any underlying issues or tensions that may have contributed to the complaint?*

14. **Preventive Measures:**

    - o *What steps do you think could be taken to prevent similar incidents in the future?*

    - o *Are there any training or resources you believe would be beneficial for improving workplace interactions?*

Additional Questions

15. **Support Systems:**

    - o *Have you sought support or advice from anyone within or outside the organization regarding the incident?*

    - o *How can the organization support you during this investigation process?*

16. Clarification and Context:

- o Are there any additional details or context you would like to provide regarding the incident(s)?

- o Is there anything else you believe the investigation committee should know?

17. Feedback on Process:

- o How has your experience been with the investigation process so far?

- o Do you have any feedback on how the process could be improved?

18. Witness Credibility:

- o Have you had any prior conflicts or issues with the complainant or respondent?

- o How would you describe your overall relationship with both parties over time?

19. Consistency of behaviour:

- o Have you observed any similar behaviour from the complainant or respondent in other situations?

- o Can you provide examples of such behaviour?

20. Motivations:

- o   Do you believe there were any motivations behind the actions of the complainant or respondent during the incident(s)?

- o   What external factors, if any, do you think might have influenced the behaviour?

21. Workplace Dynamics:

- o   How do you perceive the dynamics between the complainant and respondent within the workplace?

- o   Have you noticed any power imbalances or conflicts that might have contributed to the incident(s)?

22. Immediate Reactions:

- o   What were your immediate reactions upon witnessing the incident(s)?

- o   Did you discuss the incident with anyone at the time? If so, who?

23. Changes Post-Incident:

- o   Have you noticed any changes in the behaviour or demeanour of the complainant or respondent since the incident?

- o   How has the overall team dynamics been affected since the complaint was filed?

24. Additional Witnesses:

- o Are there any other individuals you believe the investigation committee should speak with to gain a better understanding of the situation?

- o Can you provide their contact information?

25. Final Comments:

- o Is there anything else you would like to add that has not been covered in this interview?

- o Do you have any questions about the investigation process or next steps?

Signature of Witness:

Date:

Interviewer's Notes:

- **Summary of the Witness's Statements:**

- **Observations:**

- **Next Steps:**

Confidentiality Statement

All information provided in this interview will be treated with the utmost confidentiality and will only be disclosed to those directly involved in the investigation process.

[Company Name]

[Company Address]

[Contact Information for POSH Committee]

Important Note: Please ensure to maintain separate interview sheet for each witness belonging to both the Complainant and the Respondent and ask relevant questions from the above sample questions as necessary.

POSH Investigation Report Template

[Company Name] POSH Investigation Report

Report Details:

- *Report Number:*

- *Date of Report:*

- *Investigator(s):*

    - *Lead Investigator:*

    - *Supporting Investigator(s):*

- *Department:*

- *Contact Information:*

1. Introduction:

- *Purpose of the Report:*

    o *Provide an overview of the purpose of the investigation and the scope of the report.*

- *Summary of the Complaint:*

    o *Outline the nature of the complaint, including specific allegations and the context in which the incident(s) occurred.*

- *Date of Complaint:*

- *Complainant's Information:*

    o *Name:*

    o *Employee ID:*

    o *Department:*

    o *Position:*

- *Respondent's Information:*

    o *Name:*

    o *Employee ID:*

    o *Department:*

- o   *Position:*

2. Investigation Details:

- **Date of Incident:**

- **Location of Incident:**

- **Reported By:**

  - o   **Name and position of the individual who reported the incident.**

- **Date Investigation Commenced:**

- **Date Investigation Concluded:**

- **Methodology:**

  - o   **Interviews Conducted:**

    - *List of individuals interviewed, including complainant, respondent, and witnesses.*

  - o   **Documents Reviewed:**

    - *Types of documents reviewed (e.g., emails, messages, company policies).*

  - o   **Other Evidence Collected:**

    - *Description of any other evidence collected (e.g., CCTV footage, physical evidence).*

3. Findings:

- ***Summary of Complainant's Account:***

  - *Detailed account of the complainant's version of events, including direct quotes where applicable.*

- ***Summary of Respondent's Account:***

  - *Detailed account of the respondent's version of events, including direct quotes where applicable.*

- ***Summary of Witness Accounts:***

  - ***Witness 1:***

    - *Name, position, and summary of their account.*

  - ***Witness 2:***

    - *Name, position, and summary of their account.*

  - ***Witness 3:***

    - *Name, position, and summary of their account.*

- ***Review of Physical/Digital Evidence:***

  - *Description of the physical or digital evidence reviewed and its relevance to the investigation.*

- *Timeline of Events:*

    o   Chronological sequence of events based on the gathered information.

4. Analysis:

- *Consistency and Credibility of Accounts:*

    o   Analysis of the consistency and credibility of the accounts provided by the complainant, respondent, and witnesses.

- *Corroborating Evidence:*

    o   Identification of any evidence that supports or contradicts the accounts provided.

- *Discrepancies Noted:*

    o   Description of any discrepancies between the accounts and the evidence.

- *Impact on Complainant:*

    o   Assessment of the impact of the incident(s) on the complainant, including emotional, psychological, and professional effects.

- *Behavioural Patterns of Respondent:*

    o   Analysis of any patterns or history of similar behaviour by the respondent.

5. Conclusion:

- *Summary of Key Findings:*

  - o *Recap of the most critical findings from the investigation.*

- *Determination of Harassment:*

  - o *Yes/No*

- *Explanation:*

  - o *Detailed reasoning behind the determination, referencing the evidence and analysis.*

- *Policy Violations Identified:*

  - o *Identification of any violations of company policies or legal regulations.*

- *Legal Implications:*

  - o *Explanation of any potential legal implications resulting from the findings.*

6. Recommendations:

- *Disciplinary Actions:*

  - o *Against Respondent:*

    - ▪ *Specific disciplinary actions recommended (e.g., warning, suspension, termination).*

  - o *Any Other Parties Involved:*

- *Disciplinary actions for any other individuals involved, if applicable.*

- **Remedial Actions:**

  - **Support for Complainant:**

    - *Recommended support measures for the complainant (e.g., counseling, changes in work conditions).*

  - **Workplace Policy Revisions:**

    - *Suggested revisions to company policies to prevent future incidents.*

  - **Training and Awareness Programs:**

    - *Recommendations for training programs to raise awareness and educate employees on POSH matters.*

- **Further Actions:**

  - **Additional Investigations:**

    - *Any further investigations needed to address related issues.*

  - **Monitoring and Follow-Up:**

    - *Procedures for ongoing monitoring and follow-up to ensure compliance with recommendations.*

7. Appendices:

- **Appendix A: Interview Summaries**

  - Detailed summaries of all interviews conducted during the investigation.

- **Appendix B: Evidence List and Descriptions**

  - Comprehensive list of all evidence collected, including descriptions and relevance.

- **Appendix C: Relevant Policies and Procedures**

  - Copies or excerpts of relevant company policies and procedures reviewed during the investigation.

- **Appendix D: Timeline of Investigation**

  - Detailed timeline of the investigation process, including key dates and milestones.

8. Confidentiality Statement:

All information contained in this report is confidential and should be disclosed only to those directly involved in the resolution of this matter. Unauthorized disclosure of this information is strictly prohibited and may result in disciplinary action.

Approval:

- **Reviewed and Approved By:**

- o **Name:**

- o **Position:**

- o **Signature:**

- o **Date:**

[Company Name]

[Company Address]

[Contact Information for POSH Committee]

POSH Investigation Checklist

Checklist Item	Details	Yes/No	Comments
Complaint Details	1. Date of complaint received 2. Date of the alleged incident(s) 3. Location of the alleged incident(s) 4. Names of the complainant and respondent		
Complainant Information	1. Full name 2. Position in the organisation		

	3. Department 4. Contact information		
Respondent Information	1. Full name 2. Position in the organisation 3. Department 4. Contact information		
Verification of Complaint	1. Nature of the complaint 2. Specific allegations made 3. Immediate actions taken (if any)		
Legal and Policy Review	1. Review of relevant company policies 2. Adherence to the POSH Act, 2013 3. Any legal precedents or case law relevant to the incident 4. Issue of Notices to Complainant, Respondent and Witnesses		
Documentary Evidence	1. Complaint form Emails, texts, or other written communications 2. Relevant HR records (e.g., performance reviews, previous complaints)		

		CCTV footage (if applicable) 3. *Any other relevant documents or evidence*		
Physical Evidence	1.	*Photos or videos* 2. *Objects or items related to the incident*		
Witness List	1.	*Names of potential witnesses* 2. *Contact information* 3. *Relationship to the complainant and respondent*		
Witness Statements	1.	*Written statements from witnesses* 2. *Recorded interviews (audio and video) if conducted online*		
Complainant Interview	1.	*Date and time of the interview* 2. *Questions asked and responses provided* 3. *Observations and notes*		
Respondent Interview	1.	*Date and time of the interview* 2. *Questions asked and responses provided*		

	3. Observations and notes		
Witness Interviews	1. Date and time of the interviews 2. Questions asked and responses provided 3. Observations and notes		
Incident Analysis	1. Timeline of events Consistency of statements 2. Discrepancies or contradictions in testimonies 3. Patterns of behaviour		
Contextual Factors	1. Work environment and culture 2. Past interactions between complainant and respondent 3. Potential biases or motivations		
Confidentiality Measures	1. Steps taken to protect the identities of involved parties 2. Secure handling of sensitive information		
Preventive Measures	1. Training programs 2. Policy revisions		

	3. Workplace culture initiatives		
Corrective Actions	1. Disciplinary actions (if warranted) 2. Counseling or support services 3. Monitoring and follow-up		
Drafting the Report	1. Executive summary 2. Detailed findings 3. Evidence and testimonies 4. Conclusions and recommendations		
Review and Approval	1. Internal review by IC members 2. Approval by Presiding Officer 3. Finalization and submission		
Communication with Parties	1. Informing the complainant and respondent of the findings 2. Providing support and resources 3. Addressing any concerns or questions		
Monitoring and Evaluation	1. Monitoring the work environment for changes 2. Evaluating the effectiveness of		

	implemented measures 3. Continuous improvement of POSH policies and procedures		

Presiding Officer Name

Presiding Officer Signature

Date

***Important Note:** Please note that the entire sample Templates, Notices and Checklist are created by the author of this book based on experience for easing the process of handling POSH investigations and is in no way a mandate or replacement under any sections or rules of the POSH Act.*

About The Author

Sunitha is a seasoned legal and POSH Certified Consultant with an extensive career spanning over two decades. Currently certified as a POSH Train the Trainer, she excels in contracting drafting, diversity and inclusion, employee sensitisation, and IC member training. She serves as an External IC for a few organisations. Her expertise includes drafting and reviewing critical documents used in organisations and considering the business and other risks involved in the agreements.

Previously, Sunitha held pivotal roles at ICICI Bank, HDFC Bank, Axis Bank, LawSikho, Lumina Datamatics

Pvt. Limited, Legalease Solutions LLC, LexisNexis India Pvt. Ltd, and more, demonstrating prowess in bank operations, legal operations, contract drafting, legal research, and editorial services. Noteworthy achievements include team management skills, guiding, mentoring, and training skills, managing editorial projects independently, displaying unique leadership capabilities, and impeccable problem-solving capabilities.

Rise of New Hope